Presented to:

_____

From:

_____

Date:

_____

Prayers from the Heart

© 2014 Christian Art Gifts, RSA
          Christian Art Gifts Inc., IL, USA

First edition 2014

Designed by Christian Art Gifts

Images used under license from Shutterstock.com

Printed in China

ISBN 978-1-4321-2160-0

14   15   16   17   18   19   20   21   22   23   –   10   9   8   7   6   5   4   3   2   1

PRAYERS
from the
HEART

by Karen Moore

christian
art gifts ®

*The L*ORD *is my shepherd,*
I shall not be in want.
He makes me lie down in green pastures,
He leads me beside quiet waters,
He restores my soul.
He guides me in paths of righteousness
for His name's sake.
Even though I walk through the valley
of the shadow of death,
I will fear no evil, for You are with me;
Your rod and Your staff, they comfort me.

~ Psalm 23:1-4 NIV ~

Persevere in Prayer

You've been praying all your life. Sometimes you're so close to God you feel like you could reach out and touch Him, that you could ask for anything and He would hear. Other times, you feel like you're on the opposite side of the world. You wonder if He knows that you exist and that you've prayed the same prayer for over twenty years.

This book seeks to be beside you every day, every time you bow your head to talk with your Creator. It will offer you encouragement and a sense of connection with some of the best prayers ever written, so that you realize you're not alone and that you are indeed important to the One who hears your prayers. It seeks to help you persevere in prayer, even when the odds seem to be against you, for a miracle or for a desire of your heart to be fulfilled. It shines a light so you can reflect on your situation with deeper insight and peace. It shares thoughts to carry in your heart throughout the day.

Prayer helps you sort through the opportunities of life to act on those things you feel led to pursue, to be silent when that is the greatest possible action, and to speak out when the time is right. Sometimes prayer itself is the best action you can take; sometimes God is asking you to take a new course.

As you read these prayer devotions, may they help you yield to the God of your heart, trusting in Him to answer your prayers in ways that will bring about your greatest good.

Pray without ceasing, without struggle, without worry and turn over all your concerns to your Father in heaven, for He cares for you in a personal and loving way. May God hold you in the palm of His hand and in His heart every day and always.

Prayerfully and lovingly,

Karen

January

Ask, Look, Knock

"Keep on asking, and you will receive what you ask for. Keep on seeking, and you will find. Keep on knocking, and the door will be opened to you."
~ Matthew 7:7 ~

Dear Lord, it's not always easy for me to know what to pray for, especially when I pray for a person or a cause or a situation that I do not know a lot about. Though answers may not seem apparent or issues resolved, please help me keep my heart and mind connected to You so that I can hear You. Guide me with Your counsel and open new doors of possibility.

When there are no easy answers or options, You always work on the situation brought before Your throne. I believe You know what is needed and I ask that You stay close and keep me strong. *Amen.*

Our motto must continue to be perseverance.
And ultimately I trust the Almighty will
crown our efforts with success.
~ William Wilberforce ~

January 1

Being Wise

The wise are known for their understanding, and pleasant words are persuasive.

~ *Proverbs 16:21* ~

Dear Lord, in prayer as in other matters of the mind and spirit, much of our experience rests in our perception: what we see and what we think we see. Through the gift of Your Holy Spirit, You have blessed us with the opportunity to perceive things in wise and discerning ways that may seem very different from earthly ways.

Sometimes seeing the answer to prayer is a matter of perceiving Your presence in my life and believing that You truly hear me and listen to me. The closer I am to You, Lord, the easier it is for me to understand all You have designed for my life.

Lord, thank You for giving me wisdom and understanding concerning the things that are important to me. Thank You for being so close to me as I pray.

Amen.

True wisdom is gazing at God.
~ *Isaac the Syrian* ~

January 2

Power in Prayer

Now all glory to God, who is able, through His mighty power at work within us, to accomplish infinitely more than we might ask or think.

~ Ephesians 3:20 ~

Dear Lord, You have the power to do more than I ask, more than I can imagine! When I come to You in prayer then, let me do so knowing what great power You hold over any situation in my life. I cannot measure Your power or truly even conceive of it in its fullness, but I know that the One who designed the universe by simply speaking it into being has the power to design my life. I believe You can remold and reshape me and any circumstance in which I may find myself.

God, I praise and thank You for my life and all that You are doing even now to help me. Lord, I thank You for Your powerful and loving Spirit and for shaping me in ways that only serve to make me stronger. *Amen.*

All the resources of the Godhead are at our disposal!
~ Jonathan Goforth ~

Prayers for Others

As for me, I will certainly not sin against the Lord by ending my prayers for you.
~ 1 Samuel 12:23 ~

Dear Heavenly Father, my heart is full for the needs of those around me. I ask Your kind and helping hand for those who struggle just to rise up and start again, who suffer from chronic illness and distress and who need Your comfort and love to be more visible, more real.

I ask that You be with my friends and family, my neighbors and co-workers wherever they are today, Lord, and in whatever way they may need You.

Help me always to be mindful of others and to offer help in any way that I can to serve them and to serve You more fully.

Thank You, Lord. *Amen.*

Jesus Christ carries on intercession for us in heaven; the Holy Ghost carries on intercession in us on earth; and we the saints have to carry on intercession for all men.
~ Oswald Chambers ~

January 4

Blessed Assurance

Let us go right into the presence of God, with sincere hearts fully trusting Him.

~ Hebrews 10:22 ~

Oh, Divine Spirit! Thank You for Your continual assurance of love and salvation. Whatever the world may bring my way today, remind me that You are already going before me and that You are always in control.

Help me to see Your Hand in all that I do, to share the gifts You've given me in ways that please You and to be at peace.

Only You know what I truly need today, and I rest in the assurance that You bless and guide each step I take. *Amen.*

Blessed assurance, Jesus is mine!
Oh, what a foretaste of Glory Divine!
Heir of salvation, purchase of God,
Born of the Spirit, washed in His Blood.
~ Fanny Crosby ~

Beginnings

The fear of the LORD is the beginning of wisdom; all who follow His precepts have good understanding.
~ Psalm 111:10 NIV ~

Dear Lord, whether it's a new day or a new year, You always grant us the option of starting again. Sometimes we resist beginnings, not wanting change to come into our lives, yet You know there's something healthy and beautiful about each effort we make to try again.

Today, let me begin to appreciate even more of what You mean to me and let me begin each thing I do as though I am doing it for the first time. Grant me a fresh approach, a new opportunity and the strength to keep moving closer to the goal, even if it means starting again.

Bless this day with more joy in the things You have begun in me. *Amen.*

He who chooses the beginning of the road chooses the place it leads to. It is the means that determines the end.
~ Harry Emerson Fosdick ~

Character Building

Don't be fooled by those who say such things, for "bad company corrupts good character."
~ 1 Corinthians 15:33 ~

Dear Father, I know that You want to help me build a worthy character so that I can be more of what You've called me to be. Help me not to be misled by those who are not invested in my future, but only serve to hold me back. Help me to form the kinds of habits that can sustain me for a lifetime of prayer and service to You.

You know everything about me and you have a specific plan for me. Help me to always be worthy of Your call and be willing to change when something tempts me to go down a dangerous path. I want to always build my character on the solid Rock of Your foundation. *Amen.*

My eyes will be on the faithful in the land,
that they may dwell with me; he whose
walk is blameless will minister to me.
~ Psalm 101:6 NIV ~

A Little Common Sense

"I have filled him with the Spirit of God, giving him great wisdom, ability, and expertise in all kinds of crafts."

~ Exodus 31:3 ~

Dear Lord, like the great craftsmen You gave Moses, men of wisdom and skill, I would ask for greater skill and wisdom in the things I do and say. I can act without thinking sometimes, only to regret it later. I know that to have a bit of common sense serves me well and serves You even more, so I pray today that I will have greater wisdom and genuine common sense for the gifts of my hands.

Whether I am leading others, or serving them, whether I am teaching my children or learning from them, help me to discover the lesson, the thing of greatest value in anything I might do today. In little things and big things, I pray for Your guidance and the willingness to use good common sense. *Amen.*

All should work and ask God's guidance.
~ Dwight L. Moody ~

January 8

Greater Commitment

"Because you are lukewarm – neither hot nor cold – I am about to spit you out of My mouth."
~ Revelation 3:16 ~

Father in heaven, I know that I want to fully commit my life to You and yet I also know that I have not surrendered all that I am to Your will. I ask for Your help in becoming more committed to You in every way. Guide me to understand that the more I commit to Your ways, the greater my joy will be in all that we share.

I am Your child and no matter what happens in my life, I want to be fully Yours. I pray today for Your kindness and mercy in helping me take this step. Be with all those who commit their hearts and minds to You and help each one to know You better. *Amen.*

As for me, I will declare this forever;
I will sing praise to the God of Jacob.
~ Psalm 75:9 NIV ~

January 9

Hopes and Dreams

"Your old men will dream dreams, and your young men will see visions."

~ *Joel 2:28* ~

O Lord, my God, I have so often dreamed things that have yet to come true, hoped for things that seem to elude me. Please help me to let go of any dream that is not of You, and to hold fast to the things You have planted deeply within my heart. I believe, Lord, that You have dreams to fulfill in me and through me. Let me dream the same dream so we can accomplish Your work together.

I ask You to bless all around me who seek to know more of You and Your will for their lives. Help us to desire more of what You have prepared for us here on earth. I ask for Your blessings and favor in Jesus' name. *Amen.*

Dreams do come true, if we only wish hard enough.
You can have anything in life if you will sacrifice
everything else for it. "What will you have?"
says God. "Pray for it and take it."

~ *James M. Barrie* ~

January 10

An Attitude Adjustment

Let the Spirit renew your thoughts and attitudes.
~ Ephesians 4:23 ~

Dear Father, I know that I often need an attitude adjustment. I am not always aware of slipping into unproductive and unhealthy thinking, but I know that when I realize I've done that and change my attitude about things, everything becomes more blessed again. Lord, today I pray for myself and for others, that You would inspire our thoughts, change our hearts, and help us to live more fully in Your care.

We know that with You all things are possible. With You, we have new opportunities and are safe. Help us to trust in You for all the details of our lives and to change our hearts to reflect an attitude of praise. *Amen.*

The remarkable thing is, we have a choice every day
regarding the attitude we will embrace for that day.
~ Chuck Swindoll ~

The Future Belongs to God!

"Don't worry about tomorrow, for tomorrow will bring its own worries."

~ Matthew 6:34 ~

Dear Lord, I know that I'm guilty of worrying about tomorrow and about the day after that. I ask today that You would help me to live in the present and leave tomorrow in Your divine hands. Forgive my weaknesses and grant me Your everlasting kindness.

I ask that You watch over my heart and actions and over all the people I love. Help us to be strong in faith, mindful of You in all we do, and willing to let go of worry. Strengthen our faith, Lord, and bless our lives according to Your will and purpose. I ask all these things in Jesus' name. *Amen.*

The great thing is to be found at one's post as a child of God, living each day as though it were our last, but planning as though our world might last a hundred years.

~ C. S. Lewis ~

January 12

Developing a New Habit

Can an Ethiopian change the color of his skin? Can a leopard take away its spots? Neither can you start doing good, for you have always done evil.
~ Jeremiah 13:23 ~

O Lord, please deliver me from those habits that do not serve You well. Help strengthen me, and renew my willingness to overcome those things that weaken my life. Help me to develop new habits that spill out to others with renewed energy, purpose, and joy.

I ask today that You would release all who are held captive by habits that only diminish their lives. Grant us a new vision so that we might become a new version of our former selves, a better version for the sake of others and all You would have us be. Thank You for Your grace and Your help, Lord.

Amen.

A nail is driven out by another nail.
Habit is overcome by habit.
~ Desiderius Erasmus ~

Willing to Change

"No one puts new wine into old wineskins."
~ Mark 2:22 ~

Dear Lord, You know that most of us resist change. We like things to be familiar. We like to know what to expect. If my favorite restaurant adds a new dish to the menu, I'm OK with that as long as all my old favorites are there too.

In life, though, some changes come at us so unexpectedly that we can't quite understand them, or know how to embrace them and it doesn't always matter whether those changes are good for us or not. We are simply overwhelmed when life changes too quickly.

Today, Lord, I ask Your help with accepting and embracing changes that You want for me. I ask that You would help the people I know and love with any changes that come into their lives. *Amen.*

Lord, when we are wrong, make us willing to change.
And when we are right, make us easy to live with.
~ Peter Marshall ~

January 14

Peaceful Moments

"God blesses those who work for peace, for they will be called the children of God."
~ Matthew 5:9 ~

Dear God of peace, let Your gracious Spirit descend on us and fill us with Your incredible peace. Only You can wash over us with assurance that all is well, that what we need will be provided, that what we fear will never come to pass. You know all that we need and walk ahead of us preparing the path for us.

Help us to be still, to sit in contented silence with You and trust in You for all that we need. Help us then to take our revived and peaceful spirits into all we do today so that others may be blessed. Lord, it is so easy for all of us to get swept up in the chaos of life. Help us today to step away from all that and step closer to You. In Jesus' name. *Amen.*

First put yourself at peace, and then you may
the better make others be at peace. A peaceful
and patient man is of more profit to himself and to
others, too, than a learned man who has no peace.
~ Thomas à Kempis ~

January 15

Put on a Happy Face!

A glad heart makes a happy face.
~ Proverbs 15:13 ~

Father of all joy, thank You for providing so many reasons for me to give You praise and honor. Thank You for countless blessings that fill my life with joy. You have given me all that I need and even things that are more than I need just because it gives You great pleasure to do so. You are so merciful and kind.

I ask You today to bless my family and friends with true happiness and the gift of Your ever-present Spirit.

Grant that a merry heart would replace any sense of doubt or sadness, that good news will come for those who have prayed long and hard for that news, and grant that this may be a day of great joy. I ask for Your divine favor in humble love. *Amen.*

Three grand essentials to happiness in
this life are something to do, something
to love, and something to hope for.
~ Joseph Addison ~

January 16

When I Feel Alone

"I am not alone because the Father is with Me."
~ John 16:32 ~

Dear Lord, there are days when I am not certain that anyone else "gets" who I am or why I do the things I do. When those days come, I start to feel alone and wonder if I'm still on the right track. I ask You to help me through those times, reminding me that You are always with me and that You know me better than anyone else ever could. Help me to remember the words of Jesus when He said that He was never alone because You were always with Him. Help me to trust that there is nothing I can do to be out of Your reach or out of Your love.

Bless all those who feel lonely or alone today. Give them a sense of connection, a sense of joy in knowing they are loved by You and by others. Thank You for loving each of us so much. *Amen.*

Loneliness is the first thing
which God's eye named not good.
~ John Milton ~

On Difficult Days

He will be gracious if you ask for help. He will surely respond to the sound of your cries.
~ Isaiah 30:19 ~

Dear Lord of grace and mercy, whatever this day holds, be with me. Help me to embrace the distractions and the troubles that may come, or the ones that already assail me. Help me to trust in Your mercy and the knowledge that You will be with me in every difficulty and trial.

Thank You for meeting me in the midst of struggle and filling me with renewed hope and possibility. I know that You have everything under control and that You are ready even now to help me carry the load.

I ask for Your favor this day for all who look to You for guidance and mercy. Grant us courage to move in the direction You would have us go. *Amen.*

The LORD will keep you from all harm – He will watch over your life; the LORD will watch over Your coming and going both now and forevermore.
~ Psalm 121:7-8 NIV ~

January 18

New Choices

Choose today whom you will serve.
~ Joshua 24:15 ~

Father in heaven, You have given us the freedom to make choices; You have given us an independent spirit and will. That gift often comes with difficult choices. Sometimes those choices can both seem like good options, sometimes nothing seems like a good option. Lord, please help me to choose wisely. Give me a discerning spirit and help me to make the best possible choices, whatever I do.

Help me always to choose to be a good neighbor, a good friend, and a good worker. Help me to always choose to serve You and to desire more of what You would want for me. I ask You to help me stay on the path that You chose for me. Be with those I love as they make choices today as well. I praise You, Lord, for Your love and guidance. *Amen.*

Between two evils, choose neither;
between two goods, choose both.
~ Tryon Edwards ~

January 19

I'm Sorry, Too

"I will prove to you that the Son of Man has the authority on earth to forgive sins."
~ Matthew 9:6 ~

Dear Lord, when I think about my continual need to be forgiven, I can't help but be awed by Your great love and mercy. Knowing that You forgive and then forget is even more amazing. Lord, I can't always forget the things I've done wrong even after I've asked You to forgive me.

Help me to let go of my failures in a way that gives me room to grow and change and get to the place You want me to be. When I need to be forgiven, help me to come to You and confess the matter and then move on. It's good to know that you won't hold it against me, once You've forgiven me.

I praise You for Your steadfast kindness towards me and the people who are dear to my heart. *Amen.*

God has cast our confessed sins into the depths of the sea, and He's even put a "No Fishing" sign over the spot.
~ Dwight L. Moody ~

Actions Speak Loudly

*God has given each of you a gift from His great variety
of spiritual gifts. Use them well to serve one another.*
~ 1 Peter 4:10 ~

Lord, I know that You want me to pay more attention
to the people around me. You want me to lend a hand
when I can, to use my talents for good, and to be a
loving example to others. Even though I do those
things sometimes, I'm not very consistent. Help me
to take action when I'm getting too wrapped up in
myself to think about others.

I know that You will provide for my well-being
and that You want me to do anything I can to provide
for those around me as well. Help me to remember
to pray for those in need, to donate time and money
and to speak up on behalf of those less fortunate than
myself. Help me to be a person who follows through
on the things I say I'll do to help others. *Amen.*

*I will listen to what God the LORD will say;
He promises peace to His people.*
~ Psalm 85:8 NIV ~

Growing Up

You must crave pure spiritual milk so that you will grow into a full experience of salvation.
~ 1 Peter 2:2 ~

O Lord, as much as I long to get past the stage of infancy in my faith, I know that in many ways, I am still in need of spiritual milk. I am pleased when I recognize those moments when my heart is more aligned to Your Spirit.

Father, I thank You for the ways I have grown more tender because of Your nurturing, more resilient because of Your spirit, and more devoted because of Your grace. I ask that You help me to walk with You so closely that I reflect You to others. I'm ready, Lord, for more of You and less of me. Help me to grow up in ways that demonstrate Your love to everyone on my path today. *Amen.*

There is nothing that is more dangerous to your own salvation, more unworthy of God and more harmful to your own happiness than that you should be content to remain as you are.
~ Francois Fénelon ~

Beauty Is Everywhere

Then God looked over all He had made, and He saw that it was very good!
~ Genesis 1:31 ~

Dear Lord, today I just want to thank You for the precious and beautiful things in my life. I want to thank You for the fresh winds that bring warmth to my spirit, for the lavender skies that speak of Your glory. I thank You for creating such a diverse and amazing planet for Your children to enjoy.

I thank You too for beautiful people, the ones with souls that sparkle and hearts that exude love for You. Lord, help me to offer a hint of Your goodness to others in any way I possibly can today. Help me be a reason that someone else feels the fresh breeze of Your love. *Amen.*

Ask the earth and the sea, the plains and the mountains, the sky and the clouds, the stars and the sun, the fish and the animals, and all of them will say, "We are beautiful because God made us …" This beauty is their testimony to God.
~ St. Augustine ~

Show Me the Way

If it is true that You look favorably on me, let me know Your ways so I may understand You more fully and continue to enjoy Your favor.
~ Exodus 33:13 ~

Lord, sometimes it's scary to step into today or to even think about stepping into an unknown future. The world doesn't always offer a very positive view and the darkness can be truly overwhelming. I ask that today and always, You would help me to hold firmly to Your hand, resting in Your grip, and trusting You for each step in front of me.

Please cause me to always look for You before I move on, before I try in my own way to get ahead of You. Help me to walk with You, guided by Your loving hand in all that I do. Thank You for staying close to my side and close to my heart. *Amen.*

I gain understanding from Your precepts;
therefore I hate every wrong path. Your word
is a lamp to my feet and a light for my path.
~ Psalm 119:104-105 NIV ~

January 24

Make Everything Count

I saw that there is nothing better for people than to be happy in their work.

~ Ecclesiastes 3:22 ~

Father in heaven, help me to live in the present, to take each moment You give me and make it count. I know that I often grumble about things and then give myself excuses for why I didn't accomplish more on any given day. Help me to be happy in the work I'm here to do and to live in ways that please You.

I pray today that I would be mindful of You in all that I do and that I would give one hundred percent to any task I have before me. Help me to laugh easily, to love fully, and to give from a heart that is generous and overflowing with Your love. Help me to enjoy today as the gift You intended. *Amen.*

So live that after the minister has ended his remarks, those present will not think they have attended the wrong funeral.

~ Anonymous ~

January 25

Go Confidently in the Direction of Your Dreams

"Anything is possible if a person believes."
~ Mark 9:23 ~

Dear God of all that's possible, breathe confidence into me today so that I can accomplish all I choose to do to Your glory. Help me to move quickly past obstacles that may present themselves, knowing that You have gone before me and are paving the way for greater opportunities. Help me to remember today that no matter what may happen, You are near.

When I forget that all things are possible with You, whisper Your hope into my heart again, granting me wisdom in my steps and joy and confidence. Lord, my hope and my work rest comfortably in Your hands today. Bless all those that I encounter in my walk with You. *Amen.*

Don't let obstacles along the road to eternity
shake your confidence in God's promise. The
Holy Spirit is God's seal that you will arrive.
~ David Jeremiah ~

January 26

Teach Me

Lead me, O LORD, in Your righteousness.
~ Psalm 5:8 NIV ~

Dear Lord, sometimes I feel reasonably intelligent, even clever and smart. Other times, I'm not sure I actually know anything at all. Today, I ask that You bless me with the wisdom to desire more of You. Help me to take all the clues of heaven and put them together in such a way that I can grasp the whole picture, so that I can become what You would have me become.

Our world honors and respects those who are educated. It's right to honor those things, Lord, but it's hard to imagine that they even come close to what You would desire for us to know about You. Help me to seek the kind of PhD that is Prayerful, Holy, and Divine … then I might actually discover what You would have me know. *Amen.*

Once you become aware that the main business
that you are here for is to know God, most of life's
problems fall into place of their own accord.
~ J. I. Packer ~

Tender Talk

"If you try to hang on to your life, you will lose it."
~ Matthew 16:25 ~

Dear Father, sometimes I need Your help as I look at myself. It's so easy for me to find fault with what I've done or what I haven't accomplished that I hoped to have completed by now. I wonder sometimes if I'll ever be able to become the kind of person You'd like me to be.

Today, I ask that You would help me remember to be at least as kind to myself as I might be to someone else, a complete stranger even. Help me to remember that You look at me with eyes of love and that You continue to work with me, molding and shaping me with a loving hand. Thank You, Lord, for loving me so much. *Amen.*

Turn, O Lord, and deliver me;
save me because of Your unfailing love.
~ Psalm 6:4 NIV ~

January 28

Lending a Helping Hand

Never abandon a friend – either yours or your father's. When disaster strikes, you won't have to ask your brother for assistance. It's better to go to a neighbor than to a brother who lives far away.
~ *Proverbs 27:10* ~

Lord, people everywhere need help. Sometimes I need help. When I can, I offer a helping hand and it feels good to do it. I thank You for those times when I was generous enough with my time or my resources.

Today, Lord, I ask that You would remind me that I can offer help in many ways that would please You whenever I'm willing to step outside myself and really see a need of another. I know that You want me to see them with Your eyes. Forgive me when I've been blind to the needs of others and help me to truly be Your hands and feet here on earth. I ask this in Jesus' name. *Amen.*

Even if it's a little thing, do something for those who have need of help, something for which you get no pay but the privilege of doing it.
~ *Albert Schweitzer* ~

January 29

Quiet Times

Make it your goal to live a quiet life, minding your own business and working with your hands.
~ 1 Thessalonians 4:11 ~

Dear Lord, my heart is restless without You. I know that I am often busy, sometimes even too busy for You, and so I ask today that You would walk with me in the stillness of my heart, so we can truly share some time together. I pray for Your incredible grace and peace to flow through my body so that everyone I meet today can feel Your presence as well.

I ask that You would bless those around me with Your mercy and kindness that lingers far past anything we deserve. I ask that You would forgive me when I let the noise of life intrude so much that it drowns out Your sweet and loving voice. I pray for all today who would choose to be still and wait on You. I praise and thank You, Lord, for all You do to preserve and protect me. *Amen.*

O God, make us children of quietness,
and heirs of peace.
~ Clement of Rome ~

January 30

Disappointed Again!

I looked for good, but evil came instead. I waited for the light, but darkness fell.

~ Job 30:26 ~

Dear Father, there are certainly times in life when we feel a bit like Your servant Job. We try to seek the good things, to do our best to stay strong and motivated and forward-thinking, only to sink further from the path we hope to walk. We may even feel like we've had a year or years of continual disappointments.

Today, Father, I ask that You would be especially close to all who seek You, who seek Your light and who hope in Your name. Shine Your face upon them, renew their spirits, and strengthen their resolve to rise above any circumstance that binds them to dark thoughts. Let this be a year of all good things according to Your will and purpose. *Amen.*

We must accept finite disappointment,
but never lose infinite hope.
~ Martin Luther King, Jr. ~

If I can do some good today,
If I can serve along life's way,
If I can something helpful say,
Lord, show me how.

If I can right a human wrong,
If I can help to make one strong,
If I can cheer with smile or song,
Lord, show me how.

If I can aid one in distress,
If I can make a burden less,
If I can spread more happiness,
Lord, show me how.

~ Grenville Kleiser ~

February

Take a Break!

We wait in hope for the LORD; He is our help and our shield.

~ Psalm 33:20 NIV ~

Dear Lord, sometimes I feel like I just need a break. I am continually planning and dreaming and looking for new direction, for new perspective and guidance. I want to get off the merry-go-round now and then and just breathe and yet it's hard to do.

I wonder if taking a day off causes me to impede the progress I want to make toward my goals.

Help me, Lord, to get a new perspective about the differences between taking a break and being lazy. Help me to know when to quit, at least for the day, and to resume those other activities that are good for my soul and my spirit … taking time to meditate and pray and simply relax. Thank You for Your gifts of free time. *Amen.*

Never be entirely idle; but either be reading,
or writing, or praying, or meditating,
or endeavoring something for the public good.
~ Thomas à Kempis ~

February 1

A Healing Thought

O LORD, if You heal me, I will be truly healed. My praises are for You alone!
~ Jeremiah 17:14 ~

Lord, today I just want to thank You for my healthy body. Thank You that it recovers so miraculously from stress or when I don't take time to exercise it with care. It's amazing that it heals itself of the nicks and scrapes and bruises I inflict on it.

You have designed us so incredibly that it is even hard to fully appreciate all the things our bodies do to keep us going, to keep us able to do what You've called us to do. It's no wonder that You've called our bodies Your "temple" because it is the remarkable place where we live, and the place where You live.

Lord, help me to appreciate and to take care of my body. Help me to protect it and give it opportunities for strength and renewal. Thank You for all You do to sustain me. *Amen.*

He who enjoys good health is rich,
though he knows it not.
~ Proverb ~

February 2

Mind Bending

The purpose of these proverbs is to teach people wisdom and discipline.
~ Proverbs 1:2 ~

Dear Lord, I don't always understand what passes for wisdom in our world. I wonder at the things we think to be wise when there's so much about common sense that seems to be missing everywhere. You gave us the Proverbs as a guide to wisdom, offering us insights as to what You want from us and how You expect us to behave in a variety of situations.

Sometimes we make mistakes when we trust people because they have college degrees. The more I learn about life, the more I realize that there is a lot to know and I'm still a student at best. As You walk with me today, help me to be wise in the things I do and in the choices I make. I thank You and praise You. *Amen.*

Patience is the companion of wisdom.
~ St. Augustine ~

Finding the Possible

Is anything too hard for the LORD?
~ Genesis 18:14 ~

Lord, I realize that You can do anything and that all things are possible with You. I get a little lost, however, about Your will versus my will and when we may be in sync or when You have a higher purpose for the events in my life. Though I understand intellectually that nothing is too hard for You, that all things are possible, I don't always understand how to apply that knowledge to my personal situation and how I live my life.

I ask Your help today to remain at peace about the things I don't understand. Help me believe that You always seek my best and that You have plans to give me hope and a future. I cling to Your plan and purpose for me like a ship-wrecked survivor. *Amen.*

Until we reach for the impossible
through fervent, faith-filled prayer, we
will never fulfill our created purpose!
~ David Smithers ~

First Things First

*Your heavenly Father already knows all your needs,
and He will give you all you need from day to day if
you live for Him and make the Kingdom of God your
primary concern.*

~ Matthew 6:32-33 ~

Lord, You know what a list maker I am! I do my best
to set my tasks down on paper. Of course, I'm not
always successful at getting through those lists.

I ask that You would help me to set You as my
priority each day. Help me to seek Your voice before
I step outside. Help me to realize that my days are
always a little better when I've stopped to share
some time with You first. Taking that time is not
always easy to do and sometimes even feels like it
could spin out of control. That's why I know I need
You. That's why I know I want You to be with me
every step of the way. I pray that Your Holy Spirit
would flow through me today. *Amen.*

*Commit everything you do to the LORD.
Trust Him and He will help you.*

~ Psalm 37:5 ~

People Need People

*If you think you are too important to help someone in
need, you are only fooling yourself.*
~ Galatians 6:3 ~

Lord, it seems like a lot of people need help. Sometimes it overwhelms me to think about it because
I know I don't have the personal resources to help
them all. Please remind me that You don't expect me
to take care of everyone on this planet, but to simply
be willing to do whatever I can.

I know, Father, that people have come to my aid
from time to time and I have been truly grateful.
Help me to be grateful now when I'm in a position to
do something in return. Help me to realize that there
are many ways to give and that sometimes the gifts
I can give are just those that come from a heart filled
with human kindness. Help me to reflect Your light
to those in need today. *Amen.*

*A helping word to one in trouble is often
like a switch on a railroad track ... an inch
between wreck and smooth, rolling prosperity.*
~ Henry Ward Beecher ~

February 6

Grace by Grace

Let your conversation be gracious and effective so that
you will have the right answer for everyone.
~ Colossians 4:6 ~

Lord, if there's anything I've learned, it's that I need You and the undeserved grace You so lovingly pour out upon me. I know that I can only be effective if I am gracious to others as well. I can only shine Your light if I realize that it is You who created that light within me.

Help me today to offer kind and loving conversation to the people around me. Give me wisdom in the things I say and do that I might honor You in my work and in my play. Thank You for giving each of us a life of divine grace. *Amen.*

Not only does understanding the gospel of the
grace of God provide a proper motive for us to
share our faith, it also gives us the proper motive
and means to live the Christian life effectively.
~ David Havard ~

Embrace Today

*This is the day the L*ORD *has made; let us rejoice and be glad in it.*

~ Psalm 118:24 NIV ~

Lord, I am as guilty as anyone for spending too much time regretting past events, or worrying too much about future ones. I ask that You would feed me for this day, bless this day and help me to be aware of each precious moment. Help me to use the time You have given me wisely and fully.

The older I get, it seems the days just melt into each other, and sometimes weeks go by and I start to wonder where they went. The gift of today is really all we have and so I ask You to walk with me, keeping me in the present, embracing all that You have for me. I know that with You, I can handle all that this one day will bring. *Amen.*

There is only one time that is important – NOW!
It is the most important time because it is the
only time when we have any power.

~ Leo Tolstoy ~

Apples of Gold

Timely advice is lovely, like golden apples in a silver basket.

~ Proverbs 25:11 ~

Dear Father in heaven, I love Your Word. I love that I can look to You and have confidence that I'll find the perfect text, the perfect bit of advice for the situation I'm experiencing. I know that being able to keep our word is important too. Being able to say things that uplift others and encourage them toward a better tomorrow is in some small way how we help others to hear Your voice.

Remind me, Lord, that everyone I meet needs to hear Your voice, needs to be uplifted as much as possible. No matter how anyone appears on the surface, it's possible that what they need more than anything is a "good word." Help me to always give precious words to others, like apples of gold or like light in the darkness. *Amen.*

Words which do not give the light
of Christ increase the darkness.
~ Mother Teresa ~

Goodness Gracious!

Now someone may argue, "Some people have faith; others have good deeds." I say, "I can't see your faith if you don't have good deeds, but I will show you my faith through my good deeds."

~ James 2:18 ~

Lord, I know that I have been the recipient of much kindness in my life and that many good people have come to my aid when I needed their help. I want You to know that I am truly grateful.

I ask that You keep me mindful of ways that I can pass along the light of Your love by doing good deeds, or some extended grace to those around me. Help me to offer help in any way I can and to do it with joy. I ask Your blessing on all those who are connected to me, that You might lavish Your love on their lives. *Amen.*

Since you cannot do good to all, you are to pay special attention to those who, by the accidents of time, or place, or circumstance, are brought into closer connection with you.

~ St. Augustine ~

Accepting the Things I Cannot Change

God is working in you, giving you the desire to obey Him and the power to do what pleases Him.
~ Philippians 2:13 ~

Dear Lord, thank You for loving me just as I am. Sometimes I lose sight of the fact that I'm a work in progress and that You are continually working in me to give me the desire and the opportunity to change the things that I need to change.

I praise You that You don't see a need to change everything about me, but that You already love the good parts of my life, thanks to Jesus, and that it's okay to be just as I am. I thank You that I can come before You, and even though I'm not perfect, I can offer to become a vessel of light and love to others. Thank You, Lord, for kindly shaping my life. *Amen.*

Jesus accepts you the way you are, but loves you too much to leave you that way.
~ Lee Venden ~

I Belong to You

The Lord knows those who are His.
~ 2 Timothy 2:19 ~

Dear Lord, thank You that I know where I belong, that I know where home is. Anywhere that You are, I'm home. Anywhere that You would send me, I'm still in a place where I belong because You have claimed me and made me Your own. To be honest, I cannot always comprehend what that means, how big and how wide the net of Your love is and how often You have scooped me up and protected me. You have done all these things for me, for one reason, and one reason alone … I belong to You.

I give You thanks and praise You, dear Father, for Your infinite love and deliverance and faithfulness. Thank You for giving me such a warm sense of belonging somewhere wonderful. I know that with You, I'm never too far from home. *Amen.*

I am His by purchase and I am His by conquest;
I am His by covenant and I am His by marriage;
I am universally His; I am eternally His.
~ Thomas Brooks ~

February 12

Signs and Wonders!

Jesus asked, "Must I do miraculous signs and wonders before you people will believe in Me?"
~ John 4:48 ~

Lord, I believe that miraculous things are caused by Your hand every day. I believe that You perform wonders that finite minds like mine can't truly conceive of and so I believe that with You all things are possible. I know miracles happen and that You sometimes give us very clear signs of Your presence.

Thank You for using any possible resource to help us know You, to help us be aware of Your continual presence. I believe that You are still in the miracle business. Thank You for being our God of incredible wonders! *Amen.*

It is perfectly clear that in New Testament times, the gospel was authenticated in this way by signs, wonders and miracles of various characters and descriptions … Was it only meant to be true of the early church? … The Scriptures never anywhere say that these things were only temporary – never!
~ Martyn Lloyd-Jones ~

All You Need Is Love!

Dear friends, let us continue to love one another, for love comes from God.
~ 1 John 4:7 ~

Dear Lord, I love that You love me! I love the people that are close to my heart, the people who share my life. I have to confess, though, that I'm not always clear about defining love, I'm not always certain what it really means. We strive for a willingness to love others without condition and yet, it's hard to do. I know that with You, love even for my enemies is possible. I know that all love is a matter of the heart, a matter of the spirit.

Help me to love You and to love others with my whole heart, to look to You when I'm not certain how to love someone, and to reflect You in all the ways that I can. *Amen.*

Love feels no burden, thinks nothing of trouble,
attempts what is above its strength, pleads no
excuse of impossibility; for it thinks all things
lawful for itself, and all things possible.
~ Thomas à Kempis ~

Kindly Compassion

Since God chose you to be the holy people whom He loves, you must clothe yourselves with tenderhearted mercy, kindness, humility, gentleness, and patience.
~ Colossians 3:12 ~

Dear Lord, let me learn kindness and compassion from You. Let me be willing to show all creatures tender-hearted mercy and gentleness. It's not always an easy practice. It seems that life sometimes challenge us so much that it brings out the worst in us instead of the best. Help me, Lord, to offer my best: my intervention, my care – whatever I can do to alleviate suffering.

In whatever ways I can, help me to act as Your ambassador, as a caring hand to Your precious creatures. Strengthen and renew my spirit so I might show compassion to all of Your creation, big or small. *Amen.*

Until he extends his circle of compassion to include all living things, man will not himself find peace.
~ Albert Schweitzer ~

In Need of Prayer

"If you believe, you will receive whatever you ask for in prayer."

~ *Matthew 21:22 NIV* ~

Dear Lord, there are times when I forget that the best thing I can do is stop and pray. I often think I have everything under control because I did all that I could. Father, help me to remember that the best action I can take about anything is to come before You in prayer. Help me to remember that I am continually in need of prayer.

I believe that only You know what is best for my life and that when I come to You all things are possible. Thank You for opening doors to our hearts and giving us the gifts of Your grace and mercy. Help me to pray for myself and for others with the joy of believing You will hear and answer. *Amen.*

We are all weak, finite, simple human beings, standing in the need of prayer. None need it so much as those who think they are strong, those who know it not, but are deluded by self-sufficiency.

~ *Harold C. Phillips* ~

February 16

Endurance Tests

Those who sow in tears will reap with songs of joy.
~ Psalm 126:5 NIV ~

Father in heaven, I do not always understand why there are so many hard things to overcome in this world. There are so many injustices, so much intolerance, and so little forgiveness. Help me to endure and to come to peace with my own failures. Help me to rise above those obstacles that would hinder me from accomplishing all that You have designed for me to do.

I depend on You, Lord, to strengthen me and renew me during the hard times, to lift my spirits so that I can continue on my way again, seeking the good You have for me. When I must face yet another test, be with me. Walk with me through it, carry me when I can no longer go forward on my own, and deliver me safely to the place You would have me go. Thank You for being close to me today. *Amen.*

Endurance is not just the ability to bear
a hard thing, but to turn it into glory.
~ William Barclay ~

Friend or Foe

"If you are kind only to your friends, how are you different from anyone else?"
~ Matthew 5:47 ~

Dear Lord, I like to think I'm big enough to be willing to pray for the people who offend me. The problem is, I know I don't do it all the time. I know that I harbor resentment toward people who knowingly offend me or cause pain to people I love.

Help me to love unconditionally, to see the good in others so that I might honor You and glorify You. I need Your help to strengthen my spirit and to remind me that You want me to always treat others as I would want to be treated. I pray for all those people who have caused me to suffer in any way and ask that You would bless their lives today so they might experience more joy in You. *Amen.*

That you do it willingly, pray for your enemy,
that you are glad to do it, that you are delighted
according to the inner man to obey your Lord and
pray for your enemy – this shows you are gold.
~ St. Augustine ~

The Shadow of a Doubt

The one who doubts is like a wave of the sea, blown and tossed by the wind.

~ James 1:6 NIV ~

Lord, I confess that I sometimes have doubts. They aren't doubts that You exist or that You're there for me, but more about whether I live up to what You expect of me. When I look at myself, I start to doubt why You would really care about me when You have a whole planet full of people to take care of. I start to wonder how I could have any significance at all and even whether the work I do truly matters.

Help me, Father, to realize that You value me for the faith I have in You and that You care about me beyond measure and have done so even before I was born. Help me get past those moments of unbelief and continue on the path toward being a light for You in this world. *Amen.*

Too often we forget that the great men of faith reached the heights they did only by going through the depths.
~ Os Guinness ~

Let's Faith It!

"Because of your faith, it will happen."
~ Matthew 9:29 ~

Lord, at times, it feels like I've gotten to the end of my faith, that no matter how hard I try, I can't pray any more, and I can't convince myself that faith will see me through. Forgive me for those times and help me to believe like Edward Teller did when he wrote, "When you get to the end of all the light you know and it's time to step into the darkness of the unknown, faith is knowing that one of two things shall happen: either you will be given something solid to stand on, or you will be taught how to fly."

Let me have the faith that trusts in You for all things, at all times. Bless my life with the kind of abundance that only comes from believing in You. Help me to fly! I ask You this, Father, in the name of Jesus. *Amen.*

Faith is not a once-done act, but a
continuous gaze of the heart at the Triune God.
~ A. W. Tozer ~

When It All Falls Down!

He reached down from on high and took hold of me; He drew me out of deep waters.

~ Psalm 18:16 NIV ~

Lord God, when the things in my life turn upside down, help me to know that I'm not alone, to see Your hand even then offering me peace and comfort. Help me to take the trials that come my way and turn them into blessings.

Some things are tragic, some are difficult, some are simply unexpected, and yet we know that You are in control. Help me to trust in You when all the things around me seem to be falling apart. Reach out to me and keep me steady, walking on firm ground, or if need be, grant me the ability to fly.

Be with me today and with those who call Your name all over the world. *Amen.*

Either He will shield you from suffering or He will give you unfailing strength to bear it. Be at peace, then, and put aside all anxious thoughts.

~ Francis de Sales ~

Mad as a Hornet

He will make your innocence radiate like the dawn, and the justice of your cause shine like the noonday sun.

~ Psalm 37:6 ~

Lord, I don't often get angry like a bee buzzing loudly, but I'm not good at handling things well when I am feeling outraged. Sometimes, I feel fully justified and think I have every right to be mad. Other times, I'm not even sure where the feelings come from as they rise out of me like steam from a pressure cooker.

Today, Lord, I ask You to be with me and with others who suffer the feelings of anger and don't know the best ways to help anger to pass. Give me strength and discernment to get rid of the feelings of anger and forgive a person or event that has offended me. *Amen.*

Anybody can become angry – that is easy; but to be angry with the right person, and at the right time, and for the right purpose, and in the right way – that is not within everybody's power and is not easy.

~ Aristotle ~

February 22

A Little Help
from Friends!

Never abandon a friend – either yours or your father's.
~ Proverbs 27:10 ~

Lord, sometimes I take pride in being a good person, and especially in being a good friend. I love my friends and want good things for them. Sometimes, though, I disappoint them because I can't help when they need me or I don't realize quickly enough that they are in trouble. Sometimes I talk, but I don't act to help relieve the things that trouble them.

Help me to be a good friend, a worthy friend. Help me to be there when someone needs me and to encourage them whenever possible. Keep me from only giving excuses and help me more readily to lend a helping hand. Just as You are always present, always there when I need You, help me as much as possible to be there for those who need me. I thank You for all my precious friends. *Amen.*

God has chosen us to help one another.
~ Smith Wigglesworth ~

The Strength of Ten People

I can do everything through Christ who gives me strength.

~ Philippians 4:13 ~

Lord, I come to You when I'm weak, leaning on You and looking to You for help. I come to You because You renew me and lift me up again.

Today, I thank You for giving me the strength I need to get those things done that You've called me to do. I thank You that with Your help I'm a force for good in this world. Today, I ask that You would give me the strength of ten people, so that I may please You and remain focused on those things that can make a difference to others. I pray that I will succeed in getting the job done that You've called me to do.

Amen.

The difference between a successful person and others is not a lack of strength, not a lack of knowledge, but rather a lack of will.

~ Vince T. Lombardi ~

No Worries

"Can all your worries add a single moment to your life?"

~ Matthew 6:27 ~

Lord, I don't really worry about the big things as much as I seem to worry about all the little things. Maybe I feel like the little things are more under my control. The fact is that You have everything in control. Help me to be better at leaving my life in Your hands, trusting in You for the details, and coming to You when things get out of sorts.

I ask today that You would grant me peace in all areas of my life, knowing that You are fully present. I know that any amount of worry won't change anything, but a large amount of faith can do wonders. Thank You for taking such good care of me. *Amen.*

I believe God is managing affairs and that He doesn't need any advice from me. With God in charge, I believe everything will work out for the best in the end. So what is there to worry about?

~ Henry Ford ~

Your Plans and My Plans

We can make our plans, but the LORD determines our steps.

~ Proverbs 16:9 ~

Lord, I am a planner. Sometimes that works, especially when I've been wise enough to pray first and set my goals according to Your will and purpose.

At other times, I get ahead of You and before I know it, nothing is working out the way I had planned.

Help me to stop each morning and listen for Your voice, to seek Your guidance in the things I do. Help me to desire more of Your will for my life so that my plans are in alignment with Your purposes and the steps You would have me take. I ask for Your blessing on all that I do today. *Amen.*

As we trust God to give us wisdom for today's decisions, He will lead us a step at a time into what He wants us to be doing in the future.

~ Theodore Epp ~

A Time to Sleep

People who work hard sleep well, whether they eat little or much. But the rich seldom get a good night's sleep.

~ Ecclesiastes 5:12 ~

Father, I ask that You would grant me a good night's sleep, helping my mind to rest and be at peace. So often I go to bed after a long day of working and planning and discover that my mind just won't switch off; it won't quiet down and let me rest.

Please be with me, guiding my thoughts to relax and helping my mind focus on Your strength and Your love. Help me to know that You are always with me, always seeking my good. For all Your children who need a peaceful night's rest, I ask for Your Spirit to descend on their bodies and hearts and minds. Help them to rest in Your loving care, knowing that You are fully in control. Thank You for filling our hearts with peace. *Amen.*

If you find it hard to sleep, stop counting sheep and talk to the Shepherd.

~ Anonymous ~

What the World Needs

Do not be hard-hearted or tightfisted. Instead, be generous and lend them whatever they need.
~ Deuteronomy 15:7-8 ~

Lord, the world spills over with the needs of Your children. It is hard to muffle the sounds of those crying out in great need and anguish. Those voices erupt from every corner of the globe.

Help me to do what I can. Guide me in the direction of a special organization I might support, or a needy family to whom I might offer time or money. It's so difficult to even choose where to help when there are so many hurting people. I ask, Lord, that You would make me sensitive to the needs of others so that I can help with whatever resources You have provided for me. The world is crying out for You.

Amen.

God is able to make a way out of no way, and transform dark yesterdays into bright tomorrows.
~ Martin Luther King, Jr. ~

February 28

Practice Makes Perfect!

Praise be to the Lord, to God our Savior, who daily bears our burdens.

~ Psalm 68:19 NIV ~

Dear Lord, I know that to learn anything well, I have to spend a lot of time on it, practicing until I am clear about how it is done best. It doesn't really matter what that skill is, from communicating well with others to praying regularly – I know that I have to devote time and energy to accomplish my goals. Today, I pray that You would help me focus on the things I need to do to improve. Help me to be willing to take the time to practice my skills so that I can become better at what I do.

Sometimes, Lord, I confess that I need to practice simple things like greeting others with a smile, or being willing to help. I need to practice being flexible and loving. I pray for Your help in all that I do. *Amen.*

Practice does not make perfect.
Only perfect practice makes perfect.
~ Vince Lombardi ~

February 29

Lord, You know the longings of my heart.
When I seek thrills and quick fixes to satisfy
these needs I am eventually disappointed.
Your supply of Living Water never runs dry
and satisfies the inner desires of my heart
because You are the only One
who can meet my spiritual needs.
Lord, as I come today
dry and thirsty I look to You,
for You satisfy the thirsty
and fill the hungry with good things.

~ Christian Prayer ~

March

Ah, for Some Inspiration!

Get all the advice and instruction you can, and be wise the rest of your life.
~ Proverbs 19:20 ~

Lord, oftentimes, days come and go, feeling common-place and predictable. It almost feels like a rut, like a cycle that won't be broken. Though it can almost feel like a safe place to be in, it may mean that I'm not opening my eyes to all that You would have for me. It may mean that I'm missing the step You want me to take to fulfill my greater life's purpose.

I ask that You would be with me today, inspiring my steps and watching over the things I say and do. Help me to see Your hand in all that needs to be done, to see it as an honor and a privilege to work, to play, to live, and to love for You. Bless those who seek an "aha" moment, a bit of inspiration to see them through. Help all of us to see You and to seek from You, divine moments. Thank You, Father! *Amen.*

*A moment's insight is sometimes
worth a life's experience.*
~ Oliver Wendell Holmes ~

March 1

Gifts of God

What makes you better than anyone else? What do you have that God hasn't given you?
~ 1 Corinthians 4:7 ~

Lord, I am humbled by Your kindness and the gifts You have given me. Not only have You offered me eternal life, You have given me abundant life on this earth. Here You have given me all that I possess of talent and intelligence. You have given me grace and freedom, forgiveness and joy.

If I were to start trying to make a list of all that I have because of You, I could not complete it. There would always be something I had forgotten – some blessing from a friend at just the right moment, some gift of love that would escape my memory. You, Lord, love me anyway and keep giving me even more of Your Spirit and a reason to have hope. Thank You and praise You for Your gifts. *Amen.*

An infinite God can give all of Himself to each of His children. To each one He gives all of Himself as fully as if there were no others.
~ A. W. Tozer ~

March 2

Beautiful Attitudes

There must be a spiritual renewal of your thoughts and attitudes.

~ Ephesians 4:23 ~

Father, I'm not sure what I'd be like without You. I know that I have to work on my attitude even with the kindness of Your Spirit to direct me. I know that I have to seek Your goodness and favor and realize it is always around me. You have provided for my life in every way, and the only attitude that makes sense to offer You in return is one of gratitude.

I am truly grateful for all that's beautiful, all that's meaningful, and all that's precious in my life. You are the Author of my good, the Creator of my heart and soul, and I ask that You would continue to renew my thoughts and attitudes in ways that are pleasing to You. *Amen.*

It's a beautiful world to see, or it's dismal in every zone, the thing it must be in its gloom or its gleam depends on yourself alone.

~ Anonymous ~

The Just and the Fair

Arise, LORD! Lift up Your hand, O God. Do not forget the helpless.

~ Psalm 10:12 NIV ~

Dear Lord, I know that Your intention was for our good as human beings no matter where we live on this planet. I know You created us to be strong humanitarians and to care about each other. Yet how often do we pass by a person who has been robbed and beaten by life? Why do we forget that we can be good Samaritans to each other?

I pray for Your justice to prevail in my life and in the lives of those dear to me. I ask for Your protection for the innocent, for the lost lambs of this world who are beaten down by others and for all Your precious creatures. Bless all who suffer unfairly and give them courage and peace. I pray that You would always be our Champion and Shepherd. *Amen.*

Injustice anywhere is a threat to justice everywhere.

~ Martin Luther King, Jr. ~

March 4

A Sense of Belonging

There are secret things that belong to the Lord our God, but the revealed things belong to us and our descendants forever.

~ Deuteronomy 29:29 ~

Dear Lord, I want to thank You today for giving me a real sense of belonging. Because of Your love, I realize that I am not alone in this world, but that I am in constant communication, constant protection in Your mercy. I have no doubt that I belong to You.

Thank You for all the ways we have a sense of belonging here on earth: churches, clubs, colleges. Though these can only give us a glimpse of true belonging, we feel the connection of those who join together with us for a common cause.

For those times when life feels overwhelming and when my heart aches to know that someone knows I exist, I stand in awe of You, my Creator, who has so welcomed me into Your circle of grace. *Amen.*

Human fellowship can go to great lengths, but not all the way. Fellowship with God can go to all lengths.

~ Oswald Chambers ~

The B-I-B-L-E

All Scripture is inspired by God and is useful to teach us what is true and to make us realize what is wrong in our lives.

~ 2 Timothy 3:16 ~

Father, I am so thankful for Your Word. I don't know how I would navigate the ins and outs of life without a guidebook. You have created a living work that has stood the tests of time and always comes out filling its readers with new hope and vitality.

I ask that You would bless all those who read their Bibles and give them greater understanding of You. Be with those who do not yet come to the comfort of Your grace and mercy through the Scriptures and bring someone into their lives, to help direct them to You.

Help me to share the blessings of Your love and thank You for directing my steps through Your inspired Word. *Amen.*

B-I-B-L-E
Basic Instructions Before Leaving Earth.
~ Anonymous ~

Unanswered Prayers

Devote yourselves to prayer with an alert mind and a thankful heart.

~ Colossians 4:2 ~

Lord, I confess that sometimes I get weary of praying, at least when I'm praying about the same thing over and over again. I lose confidence that You hear me. Of course, in my limited way of thinking, I simply don't understand why some prayers seem to go unanswered.

Father, forgive my lack of faith and my limited patience. Forgive me when I'm not willing to wait for You, trusting You, and believing that You have my good in mind. Help me to know that all things come together for good according to Your will.

I ask that You would answer the prayers of my heart only as You see best. Help me to trust You in all things, especially prayer. *Amen.*

I have had prayers answered – most strangely so sometimes – but I think our heavenly Father's loving-kindness has been even more evident in what He has refused me.

~ Lewis Carroll ~

Birthday Candles

Blessed are those who have learned to acclaim You,
who walk in the light of Your presence, O LORD.
~ *Psalm 89:15 NIV* ~

Lord, I know that I am not always thrilled to be having another birthday. Each of those candles reminds me that the time on earth is getting shorter and they make me wonder just what I've accomplished. Help me to know the blessing that comes with getting to light another birthday candle, the gift that it brings to begin another year.

When my birthday comes this year, help me to rejoice in all that You have given me and to remember that You still have many plans for my life. I am truly grateful for each new day and I praise You for each one You give me, knowing full well that as long as I'm on earth, I still have valuable things to do. Keep me wise and strong in Your grace. *Amen.*

Teach us to number our days,
that we may gain a heart of wisdom.
~ *Psalm 90:12 NIV* ~

March 8

Staying Awake

Then He returned to the disciples and found them asleep. He said to Peter, "Couldn't you stay awake and watch with Me even one hour? Keep alert and pray."
~ Matthew 26:40-41 ~

Lord, I know that I've fallen asleep many times, when You needed me to be awake, when You needed me to be aware of someone in need, or need simply to spend time in Your presence. I ask You to help me to stay awake, to stay alert to the people around me and the work that You would have me do.

Forgive me when I walk around in a fog of my own worries and concerns, and am asleep to all that You really have for me. Help me to wake up to all that is possible through my faith in You. I ask this in Jesus' name, *Amen.*

It is beyond dispute that some awareness of
God exists in the human mind by natural instinct,
since God Himself has given everyone some
idea of Him so that no one can plead ignorance.
~ John Calvin ~

The Blame Game

"Where are your accusers? Didn't even one of them condemn you?"

"No, Lord," she said. And Jesus said, "Neither do I. Go and sin no more."

~ *John 8:10-11* ~

Lord, I know that I am pretty good at coming up with excuses for why I have fallen short of what You expect of me. Sometimes I blame other people or circumstances. Sometimes I even blame You.

Forgive me when I do not behave in a way that is responsible. Life is full of changes and they often bring me to my knees wondering just how I got there.

Help me now to always know that You watch over me and that I am the only one to blame if I don't put all that I am or all that I dream for the future at Your feet. I ask You to be with all who pray for Your guidance that they would seek to know the truth of their own actions today. *Amen.*

The reason people blame things on previous generations is that there's only one other choice.

~ *Doug Larson* ~

Getting Smarter
All the Time

I want you to be wise in doing right and to stay innocent of any wrong.

~ Romans 16:19 ~

O Lord, we praise people who are wise and who make good decisions. We are in awe of genius at every level and in every field of science and humanity. Yet, we often do not recognize the intelligence of knowing more about You. We forget that the beginning of knowledge and wisdom comes from You.

Today, I ask that You would help me to be smarter. Help me to want to know more of You so that I can see clearly all that You have designed for my life. Let me see each person I meet as designed and loved by You.

Thank You for giving me greater wisdom in all that I do. *Amen.*

I meditate on Your precepts and consider Your ways.

~ Psalm 119:15 NIV ~

March 11

A Little Happy Dance

For the happy heart, life is a continual feast.
~ Proverbs 15:15 ~

Dear Lord, help me to embrace those moments when I feel truly happy, to savor them and remember them. Help me to never take for granted the little things that make a difference in my life and cause me to experience more joy. I ask that You would grant all of Your children little things to feel happy about. I pray that they would find important things to do for You, and that they would all know love in every possible way. Give them amazing things to look forward to. I pray for more peace and more happiness in my life and the lives of all the people I love.

You have given us the opportunity of finding happiness and of living in joy because of Your beloved Son. I pray that this kind of joy would fill the hearts of everyone I know today. *Amen.*

Happiness is neither without us nor within us.
It is in God, both without us and within us.

~ Blaise Pascal ~

March 12

Loving Your Neighbors

"Love your neighbor as yourself."
~ Matthew 19:19 ~

Father, I thank You for my neighbors. I thank You for the people who live nearby, who share the experience of life with me.

We are all living on this planet, sharing its resources, and I pray that You would help us learn how to get along, how to strengthen and renew each other wherever we are. I don't always know how to help the people in other lands who suffer from extreme poverty, but I know You do. I ask that You would raise up people to defend the poor and the innocent. I ask that You would help me to find the best ways to also care for others so that I can always be a loving neighbor at home and across the world.

Amen.

If civilization is to survive, we must
cultivate the science of human relationships –
the ability of all peoples, of all kinds,
to live together, in the same world at peace.
~ Franklin D. Roosevelt ~

March 13

Me, Myself and I

Examine yourselves to see if your faith is really genuine. Test yourselves.

~ 2 Corinthians 13:5 ~

Lord, it's a tall order to try to get rid of those things in myself that cause me to stop seeing others as You see them. You gave gifts to Your ancient theologians and philosophers that I will never have. More than that, You gave them all a mighty faith to worship You and to stand before You with their struggles in life.

Lord, I know that I put myself first far too often. I am wrapped up in my world, my dreams, my family, and my friends. Help me to step aside from those things enough to be filled with compassion for others. Help me to represent You to the people I meet each day. I ask You to help me get out of the way of the work You would have me do. *Amen.*

How good and pleasant it is when brothers live together in unity!

~ Psalm 133:1 *NIV* ~

The Green-Eyed Monster!

When Joseph arrived, they pulled off his beautiful robe and threw him into the pit.

~ Genesis 37:23-24 ~

Father, forgive us when we compare ourselves to others, coveting the things they have or the gifts You've given them. Help us to believe that You have designed each one of us for a unique purpose, no matter what our circumstances may be.

Let us not be like Joseph's brothers who misunderstood their father's love and their brother's love.

We know that jealousy does not serve us well and so I ask You, Lord, to protect us from the evils of jealous thoughts. Keep us ever close to Your side, walking in Your light so we may share all the good things You've given us with each other. Thank You for the abundance of all we have. *Amen.*

O, beware, my lord, of jealousy; it is the green-eyed monster which doth mock the meat it feeds on.
~ William Shakespeare, Othello ~

March 15

Little White Lies

"Do not lie."

~ Leviticus 19:11 ~

Father of all truth, it is heartbreaking to realize how easily little lies tumble from our lips. Oh, sure, we don't want to embarrass someone with a truth about whether we like their jacket or the way they play the guitar. Those are indeed kindnesses when we keep silent.

We do need to own up to the fact that we often tell partial truths. I might tell myself that I will exercise tomorrow and then find an excuse not to do so when tomorrow comes. I might tell myself more dangerous lies as well, ones that might keep me stuck on a path that isn't good for me.

Today, Father, I ask You to convict me of the little lies I tell myself and those I perhaps tell others. Help me to desire Your truth in all that I do. *Amen.*

White lies are non-existent, for a lie is wholly a lie;
falsehood is the personification of evil.
~ Victor Hugo ~

March 16

Taking the Lead

There were few people left in the villages of Israel –
until Deborah arose as a mother for Israel.
~ Judges 5:7 ~

Lord, I confess that I am reluctant to be a leader even when I know that You have called me to do so. I may not have to stand before an assembly and speak or direct a company to its bottom line reports, but I'm still called to lead.

I am grateful for the examples in the Bible, those men and women who rose up in a time when there were few leaders answering Your call. In a time when it was neither safe nor convenient, they answered You. They led Your people.

As I consider the opportunities to lead others this week, help me to keep my priorities in order, for I know I cannot lead wisely, unless I'm also following You. *Amen.*

You can't lead anyone else further
than you have gone yourself.
~ Gene Mauch ~

Anxious Hearts

Worry weighs a person down; an encouraging word cheers a person up.

~ Proverbs 12:25 ~

Dear Lord, it is so easy to let the little things in life become big things. I know that sometimes I create more worry simply because I don't deal with the issue at hand. Sometimes the things I worry about never come to fruition and yet I've wasted countless hours thinking gloomy thoughts.

I ask You to help me stop the noise of worry. Let me start each day with a prayer and with confidence that You are always with me. Help me to look to You when anything concerns me or makes me feel uncertain. I know that when I put things in Your hands, they are safe there and that You are far better than I am at dealing with them. Bless my work, my family and my friends. Let today be a worry-free day for all the people I care about. *Amen.*

Do not anticipate trouble, or worry about what may never happen. Keep in the sunlight.

~ Benjamin Franklin ~

March 18

Getting Stronger
Every Day

The Lord gives strength to His people; the Lord bless-
es His people with peace.

~ Psalm 29:11 ~

Father, forgive me when I refuse to come to You for strength and renewal. There are days when I am consumed with myself and feel powerless to act. When those days happen, help me to come straight to You, the Source of my strength and my possibility.

Bless my weakened spirit with Your ever-powerful one. Help me to grow stronger every day, leaning on You for all that I need. In the same way, Lord, I ask that You would bless the leaders of this country. Help them to lean on You for guidance and wisdom, so that they use their power for good in the world. Be our spirit and our sword in all things. *Amen.*

We can be tired, weary and emotionally distraught,
but after spending time alone with God, we find that He
injects into our bodies energy, power and strength.
~ Charles Stanley ~

The Possession
Obsession

"Don't store up treasures here on earth. Store your treasures in heaven, where they will never become moth-eaten or rusty."
~ *Matthew 6:19-20* ~

Lord, I often buy things for no important reason. Sometimes I simply think I need one more thing.

The truth is, I don't really need anything but You. I don't really need cupboards that overflow with things I just have to find space to store away.

As I look at the things I own, I wonder if I own them or they own me. Help me, Father, to truly keep my treasures stored in heaven. Help me to value our relationship, the love You pour out on me every day, and the people who make my life so rewarding. Help me to remember that I already have everything I need. *Amen.*

Whoever is wise, let him heed these things and consider the great love of the LORD.
~ *Psalm 107:43 NIV* ~

Nature Walk

"Where were you when I laid the foundations of the earth? Tell Me, if you know so much."
~ Job 38:4 ~

Dear Lord, it is truly amazing to me to watch the springtime flowers come back to life and to witness the rebirth of all You've created. No matter how many cathedrals we build, or how many rising architectural fortresses, nothing can compare to Your work. You who started with nothing and created everything! At best, we can only use the resources You have given us to create something new.

As I walk around today, let me pay closer attention to the things You have made: green grass, marching ants, birds that sing. It is an awesome world and You are an awesome God! *Amen.*

All things bright and beautiful,
All creatures great and small,
All things wise and wonderful,
The Lord God made them all.
~ Cecil Frances Alexander ~

Mercy Me!

The Lord our God is merciful and forgiving, even though we have rebelled against Him.
~ Daniel 9:9 ~

Dear Lord, I'm humbled by Your willingness to forgive me over and over again. Any time I come to You in prayer, seeking Your face and Your loving kindness, You're there. Thank You for never leaving me in the empty spaces of my regrets over things I've done or left undone. Thank You for picking me up each time I fall down, even when I disappoint You.

I pray for Your mercy today, on my life and on the lives of those I love in this world. Extend Your faithfulness to us, granting us Your continual mercy, and help us to become more worthy of You in all the things we do. *Amen.*

Two works of mercy set a man free: forgive and you will be forgiven, and give and you will receive.
~ St. Augustine ~

Ever Believable!

The father instantly cried out, "I do believe, but help me overcome my unbelief!"
~ Mark 9:24 ~

Dear Lord, thank You for walking with me every day. When my faith is strong, You open up new vistas for me to see, extending Your grace and mercy to me. When my faith wavers, You stand by me still, holding me up and renewing my spirit again.

You are ever believable! You are steadfast in Your willingness to receive me, even when I choose to walk blindly on my own.

Lord, I pray that You would always be my sunshine, my light that directs my steps and helps me to see more clearly all that You intend for my life. Please strengthen me, renew me and lift me up past any doubts that may work to diminish Your presence in my life. Thank You for loving me so much! *Amen.*

I believe in Christianity as I believe that
the sun has risen, not only because I see it,
but because by it I see everything else.
~ C. S. Lewis ~

Inside Out Beauty

Absalom was praised as the most handsome man in all Israel. He was flawless from head to foot.
~ 2 Samuel 14:25 ~

Dear Father, I'm not sure if we understand what it means to be a truly beautiful person. We have created a billion dollar industry that caters to keeping us looking young. We have the options to change our looks with body treatments, make-up and even plastic surgery. We are obsessed with our own images.

I pray for Your Spirit to guide us into the awareness of what true beauty really is. Though we can appreciate physical beauty, we know that inner beauty radiates in a way that nothing else can.

On those days when I am dissatisfied with the person I see in the mirror, let me reflect Your love in such a way that I would see that part of me that is special and unique, especially to You. *Amen.*

Since love grows within you, so beauty grows.
For love is the beauty of the soul.
~ St. Augustine ~

Because You Said So!

Jesus came and told His disciples, "I have been given complete authority in heaven and on earth."
~ Matthew 28:18 ~

Dear Author of my soul, You have designed me, created the manuscript that is my life and offered me a chance to play a starring role in this adventure. You have given me the option to live my life according to Your will and under Your complete authority, or to go my own way.

Father, I am grateful to be under Your loving hand, under Your complete authority. I'm happy to follow in Your ways and do all that I can to please You. Whenever I question Your authority, I hope You'll parent me with love. I know that in all of this, I have no fear because of Your great love for me and Your willingness to forgive me when I'm wrong.

How do I know all this about You? Because You said so! Thanks for the gifts that are mine because I live under Your authority. *Amen.*

The wisest have the most authority.
~ Plato ~

The Invitation

The Spirit and the bride say, "Come." Let each one who hears this say, "Come." Let anyone who desires drink freely from the water of life.
~ Revelation 22:17 ~

O King of kings, it is with a grateful heart that I accept Your invitation. I thank You for receiving me with such love and mercy. I thank You for making it possible for me to come to You when my work here is done.

I didn't have to work for the gift of Your salvation. I know that I come solely on Your faithfulness and generous invitation. I pray for all who are thirsty, who seek a way for their parched souls to be satisfied. I pray that they too would come to You, where real life begins. In Jesus' holy and precious name I pray.

Amen.

Just as I am, Thou wilt receive,
Wilt welcome, pardon, cleanse, relieve:
Because Thy promise I believe,
O Lamb of God, I come.
~ Charlotte Elliott ~

Bearing Fruit

I have fought the good fight, I have finished the race,
and I have remained faithful.
~ 2 Timothy 4:7 ~

Lord, thank You for all that I was able to accomplish today. It was one of those fruit-bearing days where a lot of things came together and I got them done. I'm happy to report this to You because I'm so often on the other side of this fence. So often, I tell You how diminished I feel for not getting things done.

Thank You for blessing me with this sense of completion and fullness. I always have a clearer picture of my life purpose when I have a day like this one.

I know You have designed me to do a particular work and I'm pleased to do it. Even more, I'm thankful when I can actually witness the progress myself of what has been accomplished. Thank You for helping me bear good fruit for You today. *Amen.*

Thou shalt ever joy at eventide
if you spend the day fruitfully.
~ Thomas à Kempis ~

Doing Things Well

*God has given each of you a gift from His great variety
of spiritual gifts. Use them well to serve one another.*
~ 1 Peter 4:10 ~

Father, if anyone gave us an example of what it means
to do things well, it's You. After all, we merely have
to look in any direction and as far as we can see are
the amazing and wonderful things You created.

I pray today that I would be more aware of how
I do any task. I pray that I would be humble enough
to be grateful that I even have a job to do, and that I'll
have enough pride in my work to want to do my best.
I pray that You would bless me with opportunities
to share the gifts You've given me, for the benefit of
those around me. Lord, it is the desire of my heart to
please You and to honor You by doing my work with
exquisite care and joy. *Amen.*

*Your greatest fulfillment in life will come
when you discover your unique gifts and abilities
and use them to edify others and glorify the Lord.*
~ Neil T. Anderson ~

March 28

I Was Born for This!

Make it your goal to live a quiet life, minding your own business and working with your hands.
~ 1 Thessalonians 4:11 ~

Lord, You are the Potter and I am the clay. You know exactly what You created me to do. Help me to discover Your will for my life so that I may please You and honor Your name. I believe I was born for a special purpose, one that only I can do. With a humble heart, I ask You to guide me.

I ask You to bless all those who search to understand how they can best serve You. I pray that You would anoint them with Your Holy Spirit, bless them with people who can help them along the way, and encourage their steps. We need Your help so that we can accomplish the very mission You want us to do. Help each of us who seek Your will to discover and answer Your call. *Amen.*

Set yourself earnestly to discover what
you are made to do, and then give
yourself passionately to the doing of it.
~ Martin Luther King, Jr. ~

Unending Supply

This same God who takes care of me will supply all your needs from His glorious riches, which have been given to us in Christ Jesus.
~ *Philippians 4:19* ~

Lord, sometimes I'm yearning so much for one particular thing, I overlook all You've done to provide for me. I thank You with all my heart for taking such good care of me. When I've had to go through difficult times and situations, You have provided friends to encourage me, the comfort of Your presence, and a sense that the future is going to be OK.

I pray that You would always supply the needs of Your children around the world. I know there is a lot of poverty and a lot of hunger. I ask today that You would feed Your children through every means possible. I ask that You would take care of my family, too, supplying the heartfelt needs of each person. Thank You, Lord, for Your great faithfulness. *Amen.*

If God sends us on stony paths,
He will provide us with strong shoes.
~ *Alexander MacLaren* ~

March 30

Drum Roll, Please!

"I am the Lord, the God of all the peoples of the world. Is anything too hard for Me?"

~ Jeremiah 32:27 ~

Father, sometimes I want to shout at the top of my lungs of Your greatness! I want all those people who are not yet listening to You to hear Your voice. I would do anything to get people to stop and look and listen to You, the Creator of this universe.

Even though life is hard and You don't always intervene when I would wish You might, I know that all things are in Your hands. I know that You are the only true source of power and that You are the God of every breathing person and creature on this planet.

I pray that those who do not know You as the one true living God would come closer to You today, that someone or something would draw their attention to You. In Jesus' name, *Amen.*

God can give only according to His might; therefore He always gives more than we ask for.

~ Martin Luther ~

March 31

*Use me, my Savior, for whatever purpose
and in whatever way You may require.
Here is my poor heart, an empty vessel:
fill it with Your grace.
Here is my sinful and troubled soul:
quicken it and refresh it with Your love.
Take my heart for Your abode; my mouth
to spread abroad the glory of Your name;
my love and all my powers for the
advancement of Your believing people,
and never allow the steadfastness
and confidence of my faith to abate.*

~ Dwight L. Moody ~

April

Wise and Foolish

There is more hope for fools than for people who think they are wise.

~ Proverbs 26:12 ~

Father, I sometimes do foolish things. I'm not always sure why, but my heart grieves when I realize I've acted unwisely. I pray that You would forgive me my foolish ways and bless me with greater wisdom.

I look to You in the hope that You would help me to grow stronger in the choices I make. Help me to resist the temptations to do things that are wrong for me, that will not benefit me in any way. Grant me a sound mind and a hopeful heart.

I ask that You would bless my life in ways that might bring honor to You. Strengthen and renew my actions and thoughts. When I act in any way that is foolish, forgive me and set me back on a right path. Help me to serve as a witness to Your love and mercy. In Jesus' name, I pray. *Amen.*

The fool says in his heart, "There is no God."
~ Psalm 53:1 NIV ~

April 1

Adversity University

Though the Lord gave you adversity for food and suffering for drink, He will still be with you to teach you.

~ Isaiah 30:20 ~

Lord, sometimes adverse situations and difficult times make me feel like a child, somewhat helpless and uncertain. In those times, You hold me up, giving me support, a place to lean in and find comfort.

I learn so much from adversity that I feel almost like a student going through a rather tough course at school. I hope if I pass all the tests and keep trying my best that I will have some opportunity to graduate from that affliction and move on.

I believe You are with me no matter what I must face in this life and I thank You for Your kindness and Your guidance. Only with You can I hope to be made strong. Only with You can I look to grow into the person You want me to be. *Amen.*

Afflictions are but the shadows of God's wings.
~ George MacDonald ~

April 2

Simple Devotion

*You must fear the L*ORD *your God and worship Him and cling to Him.*

~ Deuteronomy 10:20 ~

Dear Lord, I am humbled by Your steadfast love, Your patience, and Your willingness to stay close to me. Though my finite mind can hardly comprehend all that You are, I am grateful to know that You are there any time I turn to You.

Today, Father, I ask You to bear with me, comfort me, and hold me in Your loving grasp, for my heart craves You, believes in You, and trusts You. I pray that I might fully devote myself to Your service, Your generosity, and Your guidance for all that I am and all that I hope to be.

Bless my simple-hearted devotion to You, for it is all I have to give. *Amen.*

Lord, make me according to Thy heart.
~ Brother Lawrence ~

Seeds of Hope

All praise to the God, the Father of our Lord Jesus Christ.
It is by His great mercy that we have been born again.
~ 1 Peter 1:3 ~

Lord, I confess that my faith is sometimes weak. You have planted the seeds of hope in my soul and I long to watch them grow. I know that it is only because of You that I have any reason to hope in the future, any reason to rejoice in the present day.

You know what You designed me for, what You desire of me, and what You planned for me even before I was born. Now that I am born again in You, help me to be renewed by Your grace and strengthened by Your Spirit. Help me to become the fruitful follower who brings happiness to others and pleases You as well.

I ask for Your loving hand to always rest upon my soul and my spirit. In Jesus' name! *Amen.*

If seeds in the black earth can turn into such
beautiful roses, what might not the heart of man
become in its long journey toward the stars?
~ G. K. Chesterton ~

Making a Little Music

Come, let us sing for joy to the Lord; let us shout aloud
to the Rock of our salvation!
~ Psalm 95:1 NIV ~

O Lord, You have indeed filled our hearts with the sounds of music! You have blessed us with favorite hymns that fill our spirits with the grace of Your gospel. You have calmed our souls with gentle melodies.

I thank You for all these gifts of music and the variety of ways music is expressed around the world. I know that one day, Lord, we will all gather around Your throne and sing to our hearts delight in praise to You. Until that day, give us reasons to sing and opportunities to rejoice in all that we have because of Your kindness. Bless those we love today and let their hearts sing with joy for all You've done in their lives. You are an awesome God! *Amen.*

Music is the perfect way to express our love
and devotion to God. It is one of the most magnificent
and delightful presents God has given us.
~ Martin Luther ~

Help!

*My help comes from the L*ORD*, the Maker of heaven and earth.*

~ *Psalm 121:2* NIV ~

Father, sometimes the strongest prayer of my heart comes out in one word: "Help!" I don't always know what I need, I just know I need You and I need Your guidance. Today, I pray for the help that only You can give me, the help that fills my heart with hope and renews my sagging spirit.

Help me to stick close to Your side, to be mindful of You in all that I do, and to seek opportunities to show Your great love to others. As You help me, may I be willing to help those around me.

I thank You for the help You've always given me and ask You once again to draw near to me as I long to have Your counsel and advice. I praise You and thank You. *Amen.*

Save us and help us with Your right hand,
that those You love may be delivered.
~ *Psalm 60:5* NIV ~

Grace and Gratitude

Be thankful in all circumstances, for this is God's will for you who belong to Christ Jesus.
~ 1 Thessalonians 5:18 ~

Lord, I doubt I could list all the reasons I'm grateful to You. I could count my blessings far longer than those things that trouble me. You provide for my life with an abundance that I will never understand or deserve. You give me the continual gifts of Your forgiveness, salvation, peace, and mercy. You give me things that no money could ever buy.

This world so often makes it difficult to remember the gifts of grace and possibility that knowing You brings. I can get caught up in collecting things, paying bills and balancing ledgers, and forget that none of that truly matters. Without Your grace and mercy, I have nothing at all. Today, Lord, I thank You with all my heart for the gifts and treasures that only You can bring to my life. *Amen.*

Gratitude is the fairest blossom
which springs from the soul.
~ Henry Ward Beecher ~

April 7

To Life!

In Him we live and move and exist. As some of your own poets have said, "We are His offspring."
~ Acts 17:28 ~

Lord, there are days when we seem to look at life, yawn and wonder how we got here. Other days, we're so full of life we hope it goes on forever. You have agreed to give us life and to sustain us so that we can live and breathe and move. In You, we know we exist.

Father, thank You for this life! Thank You for the incredible moments when we connect to You in ways we cannot put into words. Thank You when we connect in love to others. More than anything, let me always remember to live it fully, not taking even one moment for granted. I praise You and thank You for my life. *Amen.*

The life of the individual only has meaning only insofar as it aids in making the life of every living thing nobler and more beautiful. Life is sacred, that is to say, it is the supreme value to which all other values are subordinate.
~ Albert Einstein ~

April 8

The Gospel Truth

Satan, who is the god of this world, has blinded the minds of those who don't believe. They are unable to see the glorious light of the Good News.
~ 2 Corinthians 4:4 ~

Father, thank You for giving us the gospel truth! Thank You for Your Son, Jesus, who gives us the way to draw near to You and the purpose for which we were born.

For all of those who think Your laws were for ancient peoples or who have not yet discovered the truth for themselves, I ask Your favor. I pray that You would intervene in their lives and show them who You are so they can come to know You and love You.

My spirit rejoices in knowing I can come to You just as I am. Thank You for loving all of Your children so well. *Amen.*

The gospel has lost none of its ancient power. No human device need be tried to prepare the sinner to receive it, for if God has sent it no power can hinder it; and if He has not sent it, no power can make it effectual.
~ Dr Ethelbert W. Bullinger ~

Gifted People

He has given each of us a special gift through the generosity of Christ.

~ Ephesians 4:7 ~

Lord, I will confess that I don't always understand Your amazing gifts. I'm almost certain I don't utilize them as fully as I could and obtain the benefits You intend. I even worry that You might not think I appreciate what You've done, but I truly do.

With my finite mind, I can't really imagine what it means to have ever lasting life, nor do I feel especially holy, but I am grateful always that You accept me as I am. I believe that You know everything about me and that You accept the gifts I return to You, as humble as they are. Thank You, Lord, for Your grace and continual generosity and love. You give me more than I can ever deserve. *Amen.*

How blessed and wonderful, beloved, are the gifts of God! Life in immortality, splendor in righteousness, truth in perfect confidence, faith in assurance, self-control in holiness!

~ First Epistle of Clement ~

April 10

Blue Sky Days

Are any of you happy? You should sing praises.
~ James 5:13 ~

Lord, it's a blue sky day! Everything feels like a breath of fresh air and a ray of sunshine today. Does that mean I've given up all my worries? Of course, You know You'd like me to do that, and I probably haven't done it all the way, though I gladly surrender them to You now.

It just means that I know how precious each day is and I believe You want the best for me. I know that You work hard to help me see the best path to take in this life and that You have blessed me beyond measure.

Father, I thank You for days like this when I can feel Your presence in every place I walk, in everything I do, and on the face of each person I meet. It's a beautiful day, Lord, any time I can spend it with You. *Amen.*

The happiness of the creature consists in rejoicing in
God, by which also God is magnified and exalted.
~ Jonathan Edwards ~

April 11

A Simple Form of Art

It is pleasant to see dreams come true.
~ Proverbs 13:19 ~

Dear Lord, I may never be an artist in the true sense of the word. I won't be creating masterpieces on the Sistine Chapel or carving enduring statues of bronze, but I know You've given me some artistry.

You've given me an eye that appreciates the beautiful things I see whether they are made by Your heavenly hands, or by one of Your children. You've given me an artistic heart that keeps on dreaming and hoping and believing that all things are possible with You.

I know that my gifts are some kind of simple art form, but they enrich my life nevertheless. Thank You for giving me such incredible gifts. *Amen.*

*The true work of art is but a
shadow of the divine perfection.*
~ Michelangelo ~

Silence Is Golden

Set a guard over my mouth, LORD; keep watch over the door of my lips.

~ Psalm 141:3 NIV ~

Lord, I really love the quiet times, when I don't even have to speak, but I know we are still talking. I love to sit in Your presence and drink in the silence. It fills my spirit in so many ways. Thank You for leading me beside the still waters and knowing when I just need to quiet down.

I know that when I don't take time to be alone with You. I start believing I'm doing all right on my own. I know that in those times, it would be better for me to stay still, to be silent, and not be thought foolish. When I forget to be quiet, please remind me and help me to find all my strength and wisdom in You. *Amen.*

Silence is the mother of prayer. It frees the prisoner; it guards the divine flame; it watches over reasoning; it protects the sense of penitence.
~ St. John Climacus ~

A Clinging Vine

Cling to your faith in Christ, and keep your conscience clear.

~ 1 Timothy 1:19 ~

Dear Vinedresser, I know that You see me, since I hold on to You for dear life. If I don't hold on to You, life is not as dear, not as meaningful, not as grace-filled. You are the One who directs my steps, prunes those sprouts of doubt and mistrust that try to grow up inside me. You are the One who keeps me skillfully growing to become all that You've designed me to become.

As You watch over the gardens all over the world that contain Your own dear children, please help them cling to You wherever they are. It's such a joy to know how well You tend Your gardens, not wishing that any be deprived of coming to full bloom. Thanks for being such an attentive gardener! *Amen.*

Faith is something that is busy, powerful and creative, though properly speaking, it is essentially an enduring more than a doing. It changes the mind and the heart.

~ Martin Luther ~

April 14

Life Can Be So Taxing!

Our present troubles are small and won't last very long. Yet they produce for us a glory that vastly outweighs them and will last forever!
~ 2 Corinthians 4:17 ~

Father, it's been one of those days! Nothing seems to have gone the way I had hoped. My to-do list is going to be exactly the same tomorrow. Please help me to get back on track and to get past the obstacles that keep me from accomplishing my goals.

I know that only You can truly direct my steps and so I turn to You once again and ask You to be with me as I go forward. Be my Strength and my Guide, my Protector and my Guardian. I ask that You would also be these very things for the people I love most in this world. We all need You, Lord, and when life seems to tax every nerve and every fiber of our being, we need You more than ever. Thanks that I can always come to You. *Amen.*

In times of affliction we commonly meet with the sweetest experiences of the love of God.
~ John Bunyan ~

Love Your Neighbor

"Love your neighbor as yourself."
~ Leviticus 19:18 ~

Lord, each morning when I rise, I rejoice in knowing You are near. In sunshine and in rain, Your presence brings the light into my life. Thank You for adding the brilliance and the inspiration to all I do.

Today, Lord, I pray especially for the people in my neighborhood. I don't know what the issues might be, their concerns, their joys, but I do know that whoever they are, they need Your support and comfort. I ask that You would bless the ones I know and the ones I've yet to know with Your everlasting light and love.

Fill my heart with love for people that are strangers to me today and help me bring them into my circle of friends tomorrow. *Amen.*

There is no principle of the heart that is more acceptable to God than a universal, ardent love for all mankind, which seeks and prays for their happiness.
~ William Law ~

April 16

Grant Me Insight

Test everything that is said. Hold on to what is good.
Keep away from every kind of evil.
~ 1 Thessalonians 5:21-22 ~

Lord, I know that part of me likes to believe in magical thinking. I like to believe the best about people and situations and expect only the good. Because of that tendency, I sometimes find myself baffled when someone deceives me intentionally, giving me false information and hoping to keep me from the truth.

I ask You to protect me from those people and give me a truly discerning spirit so I may know the truth. Help me to never deceive someone else either so that I am worthy of Your love and respect as well.

Sometimes the world tosses up a lot of smoke and mirrors and without Your help, we can be taken in and left to bear the consequences. Help me and those I love to be more discerning today. *Amen.*

Many are the woes of the wicked, but the LORD's
unfailing love surrounds the man who trusts in Him.
~ Psalm 32:10 NIV ~

Obstacle Courses

*The angel of the L*ORD *encamps around those who fear Him, and He delivers them.*

~ Psalm 34:7 NIV ~

Father, some days it feels like I'm simply running through a maze, some kind of bizarre obstacle course. Nothing I intend comes together and everything takes twice the amount of time and effort to accomplish. It's amazing that I get anything done.

I wonder if You feel that way about me sometimes. Do I put so many obstacles in the way of Your love and guidance that I keep falling down because I can't see You clearly? If I do that, I ask that You would help me to stop, wait, and not move until I get clear direction from You.

I know that my life is fixed on You and You're my guiding star. Help me to stop looking at the obstacles and look only to You. *Amen.*

One who gains strength by overcoming obstacles possesses the only strength which can overcome adversity.

~ Albert Schweitzer ~

April 18

A Little Confession

If we confess our sins to Him, He is faithful and just to forgive us our sins and to cleanse us from all wickedness.

~ 1 John 1:9 ~

Lord, I'd be the first to admit, I don't always get things right and I don't always do right. My heart is in the right place most of the time, but I don't always follow through as I should.

Today, I ask that You would help me by strengthening my resolve to do better, to try harder, and to do the right thing, no matter how hard. Help me to not deceive even myself, but to seek Your help when I get lost.

I lay down my weaknesses before You now and ask that You would come to me in Your strength and renew my heart and mind. Forgive me for all the little sins of commission and omission that I have done in the past few days. *Amen.*

*We must lay before Him what is in us,
not what ought to be in us.*
~ C. S. Lewis ~

April 19

It's So Comforting!

He comforts us in all our troubles so that we can comfort others. When they are troubled, we will be able to give them the same comfort God has given us.
~ 2 Corinthians 1:4 ~

Lord, I bask in Your goodness! I rest in Your comforting arms knowing that I am never far from Your watchful eye. Thank You for loving me so much that You would spread Your wings like a mother hen and keep me close to Your side.

As I go through the day, remind me of those around me who need special comfort as well. Let me share with them the joy of feeling safe and secure, of feeling cared about and loved.

Remind me that uncomfortable moments are opportunities for me to draw closer to You, to seek Your grace and mercy, knowing that with a loving heart You will embrace me. Praise You, Lord, for Your unending mercy. *Amen.*

God does not comfort us to make us comfortable only, but to make us comforters.
~ John H. Jowett ~

The Cross of Calvary

He was pierced for our rebellion, crushed for our sins.
He was beaten so we could be whole. He was whipped,
so we could be healed!

~ Isaiah 53:5 ~

Father of grace and mercy, ever since we first met, I've been trying to understand just what You did that day at Calvary. Though I can understand the historical account, I'm not sure my spirit truly takes in what You did. I wonder why You did it! If I try to imagine that You knew even then that someday, I'd come along and need You, well … that's amazing to me.

I know that I'll never feel worthy of Your sacrifice, but I hope You know that my heart longs to be what you want me to be. My soul weeps with joy over the incredible step You took on my behalf. So, in case I never said it before, today, I just want to say … Thank You, Father! Thank You! *Amen.*

The cross is God's truth about us, and therefore it is
the only power which can make us truthful. When we
know the cross we are no longer afraid of the truth.
~ Dietrich Bonhoeffer ~

April 21

Jiminy Cricket

My conscience is clear, but that doesn't prove I'm right. It is the Lord Himself who will examine me and decide.

~ 1 Corinthians 4:4 ~

Lord, thank You for putting such a conscious part of Yourself within us so that we always can know how to make good choices. When I think back on the story of Pinocchio and his conscience in the form of Jiminy Cricket, it reminds me how easy it is to get off the track.

I ask Your help in being willing to listen more closely to my conscience, to that still small voice that comes from Your Spirit. I ask that You would help all people trust so much in You that no other voice could tempt them away from You. As I go about my day, Lord, let me please You by honoring the voice of Your guidance as it radiates through my mind and heart. *Amen.*

Conscience tells us in our innermost being of the presence of God and of the moral difference between good and evil.

~ Billy Graham ~

April 22

With Fear and Trembling

The Lord is my light and my salvation – whom shall I fear? The Lord is the stronghold of my life – of whom shall I be afraid?

~ Psalm 27:1 NIV ~

Father, I know that You are not the author of the timid, but the Creator of the strong and the brave. Please help me to trust in You to such a degree that no fear would be insurmountable and no obstacles too difficult to overcome.

I know that many fearful things happen in the world and my heart grieves for those in that kind of forbidding atmosphere. Help Your children, Lord, wherever they may be, to stand strong and deliberate in You. Whatever I have to face today and in the days ahead, let me do it knowing that You are with me. I draw my courage from Your grace and mercy. *Amen.*

We gain strength, and courage, and confidence by each experience in which we really stop to look fear in the face … we must do that which we think we cannot.

~ Eleanor Roosevelt ~

What Will Be, Will Be!

Teach me Your way, LORD, that I may rely on Your faithfulness; give me an undivided heart, that I may fear Your name.

~ Psalm 86:11 *NIV* ~

Lord, forgive me when I complain about little matters from day to day. Help me to stand so closely by Your side that nothing can come between us and the peace that Your Spirit brings to my life.

Help me to surrender my need to be right, or my desire to be noticed, or my hope to be praised. Give me a humble heart and an attitude of true acceptance over each situation in my life, whether I understand all the aspects of it or whether I don't.

I recognize that when I complain, it's often because I expected more of someone else, or more of myself, or even more of You, but Lord, I know that complaining does not serve You well. Today, I surrender myself and my will to You. *Amen.*

*The greatness of a man's power
is the measure of his surrender.*
~ William Booth ~

April 24

Success Secret

*As long as the king sought guidance from the LORD,
God gave him success.*

~ 2 Chronicles 26:5 ~

It sounds so simple, Lord, to imagine great success because I've acknowledged You. It sounds simple, but it is not really that easy. I admit that a lot of the time, I go ahead without You, doing the things I think I should do, but not really stopping to seek Your advice.

I also know that I often find myself a long way from the outcome I had hoped for because I did it my way, instead of checking to discover more about Your way. Help me to seek You more carefully and more thoughtfully and more prayerfully from now on.

I long to be Your servant, Your child, and Your ambassador here on earth in any way I can. Thank You for Your great love for me. *Amen.*

*The secret of my success? It is simple.
It is found in the Bible, "In all thy ways
acknowledge Him and He will direct thy paths."*

~ George Washington Carver ~

April 25

A Sense of Purpose

God has sent me here to keep you and your families alive and to preserve many survivors.
~ Genesis 45:7 ~

Dear Jesus, I long to fulfill my life purpose, that reason for which I was designed. I believe that You sent me here with an intention to do good in some way, to share a positive spirit, to honor others and to live a life of peace and grace. I also believe that You have a very specific job in mind for me.

Help me to always seek to know more of that purpose. Help me desire always to come closer to You so that I might not let my life pass by without completing my sense of mission. You know who I am, what I am, and what I can do. I look to You to guide me every day in ways that would bring me into alignment with Your will. Thank You for giving me a joyous sense of purpose. *Amen.*

The main thing in this world is not being
sure what God's will is, but seeking it sincerely,
and following what we do understand of it.
~ Paul Tournier ~

Daily Prayers

"I tell you, you can pray for anything, and if you believe that you've received it, it will be yours."
~ Mark 11:24 ~

Dear Lord, I long to be a prayer warrior. I want to be in continual communication with You. When I rise in the morning, I want my first thought to be of You.

In the evening, I want to recall the day with gusto and thanksgiving for the opportunities and the challenges that we faced together. I want to walk with You, talk with You and never get ahead of You wherever we have to go.

I pray today that I would become a strong person of prayer and that I would never forsake the chance You have given to each of us to spend time in Your presence. Help me to see You everywhere I go so that I can shine a light for others to desire more of You as well. Hear my prayers today and always, Lord, because of Your great faithfulness. *Amen.*

Prayer is the key that opens to us the
treasures of God's mercies and blessings.
~ Henry Ward Beecher ~

Simply Divine

*We know that God causes everything to work together
for the good of those who love God.*
~ Romans 8:28 ~

Lord, I know that everything about You is simply
Divine! You are the Provider, the Counselor, the
Savior, the merciful One, the Forgiver, and all else
that I could need. Only You hold the fate of this
world and the next in Your hand.

I'm so grateful to know that no matter how many
times I might botch things up, You will always be
there, ready to help. You know what I need and how
to turn evil into good. I thank You and praise You for
Your unending love and incredible patience.

I ask that You would watch over Your children
wherever they are and provide for their needs. Open
the hearts of people who can help relieve someone
else's burdens. Help us be Your hands and feet on
this planet every chance we get. *Amen.*

*A firm faith in the universal providence of
God is the solution for all earthly problems.*
~ B. B. Warfield ~

Planting New Seeds

Grow in the grace and knowledge of our Lord and Savior Jesus Christ.
~ 2 Peter 3:18 ~

Lord, help me to plant new seeds for my life in more fertile soil. Direct my steps so that the things I do can take root and grow well in Your care and keeping.

I know that sometimes I resist You when I'm stubborn. Only You can know when to prune the direction I'm taking, and fertilize new possibilities, for only You know all that You designed me to be.

Today, Father, I ask that You would be my consummate Gardener, nourishing me, granting me both rain and sun according to Your will and purpose for my life. Renew my spirit so that I might grow stronger in Your love and in my awareness and knowledge of You. I ask that Your favor may be reflected in my life and the lives of those I love. *Amen.*

All growth that is not toward God,
is growing to decay.
~ George Macdonald ~

For the Love of Reading

Create in me a pure heart, O God, and renew a
steadfast spirit within me.
                    ~ Psalm 51:10 NIV ~

Lord, I am so thankful for all the authors and writers You've created in this world. I especially love to read those books that give me a greater awareness of You and a clearer sense of who You are.

Father, thank You for books and especially for Your Word. It is such a powerful guide to living on earth. Thank You for inspiring the ancient writers so that generations could benefit from all that they learned of You.

Help all of us who seek to know You better, to be inspired by the words of those You've anointed to help us along the way. I ask Your special blessing on those writers and speakers today. *Amen.*

Christian devotional reading helps
us find intimate union with God.
              ~ Jonathan Edwards ~

I asked for strength, that I might achieve;
I was made weak, that I might learn humbly to obey.
I asked for health, that I might do greater things;
I was given infirmity, that I might do better things.
I asked for riches, that I might be happy;
I was given poverty, that I might be wise.
I asked for power, that I might have the praise of men;
I was given weakness, that I might feel
the need of God.
I asked for all things, that I might enjoy life;
I was given life, that I might enjoy all things.
I was given nothing I asked for,
but everything that I hoped for.
Despite myself, my prayers were answered;
I am among all men most richly blessed.

~ A Confederate Soldier's Prayer ~

May

Power Builders

Now all glory to God, who is able, through His mighty power at work within us, to accomplish infinitely more than we might ask or think.

~ Ephesians 3:20 ~

Almighty God, I thank You that You have blessed my life so enormously. You have not only provided for all my physical needs, but You have given me an opportunity to plug into You as a source of all power.

Your power leaves me baffled and awed. You created a world out of nothing. You created life from the dust of the ground and You sustain life by Your own will.

Lord, on my own, there is little I can accomplish. I am not built in a way that gives me the strength to do anything worthwhile without being plugged into You. Thank You for receiving me and for loving me without condition, but simply out of great mercy because of Your Son, Jesus. I am humbled by Your glorious presence and awed by Your power. *Amen.*

With the power of God within us,
we need never fear the powers around us.
~ Woodrow Kroll ~

May 1

You've Got Great Potential!

Your hands made me and formed me; give me under-standing to learn Your commands.
~ Psalm 119:73 *NIV* ~

Lord, I know that You have given me some great gifts and if I just meet You half way those gifts will serve both of us well. The funny thing about having potential is that it's not always easy to live up to it.

I want to thank You though because You always treat me as though I can do anything. You put a lot of responsibility in my hands and You honor me enough to let me find my way to achieving Your goals. Because You believe in me, Lord, I want to try harder.

Someday I want to be able to tell You how glad I am that I pushed through my weaknesses and became Your trusted friend. Thanks for giving me such great potential! *Amen.*

Continuous effort – not strength or intelligence – is the key to unlocking our potential.
~ Winston Churchill ~

May 2

Hold Your Horses!

I wait for the Lord more than watchmen wait for the morning, more than watchmen wait for the morning.
~ Psalm 130:6 NIV ~

Lord, here I go again, just chomping at the bit, ready to run off and do things on my own. How many times will I have to deal with the lesson, that when I do things without You, they never come out as I had hoped and they often leave me in a tangled up kind of mess?

Please be with me today and help me to be patient. Help me to wait for You before I act on matters that are important. Help me to be willing to walk and not just run when I need to be more careful about the results of things I do.

Take the reins of my life and help me to move along at a quiet, worthy pace so that I can do all things well for Your glory. *Amen.*

It is hard to wait and press and pray, and hear no voice, but stay till God answers.
~ E. M. Bounds ~

May 3

A Further Quest

The fear of the LORD is the beginning of wisdom; all who follow His precepts have good understanding.
~ *Psalm 111:10 NIV* ~

Lord, I'm grateful that You have given me a discerning heart and a questioning mind. Sometimes I actually need to ask more questions than I do so that I can discover the truth in a situation more quickly.

I pray today that You would help me know when to ask questions. Help me to enjoy the questions and the quest for truth as much as I enjoy getting to the right answer.

You know what is best for me and so I seek Your guidance in all ways that I may be wise in the things I do. Many people claim to have some aspect of Your truth. Some even claim to have the only truth, but Lord, I believe the only truth comes from You. Help me to always seek that truth above all else. *Amen.*

A prudent question is one half of wisdom.
~ *Francis Bacon* ~

May 4

It's the Principle
of the Thing

*I will maintain my innocence without wavering. My
consciene is clear for as long as I live.*
~ Job 27:6 ~

Father, I pray that I would always live up to the
principles that set me apart from the world and bring
me closer to You. I don't always recognize Your ways,
but I always seek to follow You as closely as I can.

When I compare myself with others, I sometimes
lose my way, my own truth, because I wonder if they
have found a better way, and yet, Lord, I know the
truth. There is no better way than the one You offer.
You are the guiding principle of my life and I am
bound to You.

Please be with all Your children who seek the ab-
solute truth that only You provide. Help all of us to
stand for what we believe in so that others may see
the light of Your love within us. *Amen.*

I have trusted in the LORD and have not faltered.
~ Psalm 26:1 NIV ~

A Humbling Experience

If you think you are standing strong, be careful not to fall. The temptations in your life are no different from what others experience.
~ *1 Corinthians 10:12-13* ~

Lord, I confess that sometimes I do have the wrong kind of pride. I know that I can set myself apart from others without really realizing that I've done so. I can assume that my life or my work or my thoughts are more important or more needed in this world than the thoughts of someone else.

It's always good for me to stop and remind myself to count my blessings and step aside from any thought of human praise or notoriety. I ask Your help in this because I want to please You in all that I do.

Thank You for loving me so much, even when I puff up a little more than I should because of what little I do well. You alone are my Source, my love and my light. *Amen.*

Whom have I in heaven but You? And earth has nothing I desire besides You.
~ *Psalm 73:25 NIV* ~

People Power

For you are children of God through faith in Christ Jesus.

~ Galatians 3:26 ~

Lord, You have created some extraordinary people! Sometimes I'm awed at the gifts and talents You have unveiled in those who make such a difference in this life. I watch talent shows on television, or I see performers who shine for You and I am impressed with the abilities You've given us.

Sometimes I forget that everyone is extraordinary to You. Everyone has a talent that You are aware of even if the rest of us are not. We are all Your children and therefore we're part of the same family.

I pray that You would help me embrace each person I meet with the light of Your glory. Help me to be willing and able to see all people as You see them … with love and grace. *Amen.*

I praise You because I am fearfully and wonderfully made;
Your works are wonderful, I know that full well.
~ Psalm 139:14 NIV ~

Once upon a Time

"From eternity to eternity I am God. No one can snatch anyone out of My hand. No one can undo what I have done."

~ Isaiah 43:13 ~

Lord, thank You for this new day. Thank You that when I fall asleep at night, I can fully expect to rise again the next day, because You hold eternity in Your hand. I pray that You would help me to have more respect for the whole idea of time.

Help me to not waste time or let it escape me as though I had time without limits. When I was a child, I thought I had lots of time. Now time is fleeting and I find myself wishing I could gather the moments up in my arms and hold on to them. Alas, I cannot for You own the gift of time. Only You know the days and hours of a person's life. Thank You for this incredible gift of time and of years You have given me. Grant that I may always be wise in how I spend these precious moments on earth. *Amen.*

In God, time and eternity are one and the same thing.
~ Henry Suso ~

May 8

Just What I Thought

"My thoughts are nothing like your thoughts," says the Lord. "And My ways are far beyond anything you could imagine."

~ Isaiah 55:8 ~

Lord, it's funny how many times something will turn out exactly as I thought it would. If I projected that it might go badly, it did. If I projected that it would go well, it did. Of course, things went contrary to my thoughts just as often.

I pray that You would nourish the ideas and the insights that come to me so that I could shine Your light and glorify You.

I know that there is great truth to the idea that thoughts themselves are very powerful and that we need to form our thoughts carefully. If we walk around carrying the wrong thoughts or information, we can do a great deal of harm to ourselves or to others. Lord, bless my thoughts today and if possible, align my thoughts to Yours. *Amen.*

You perceive my thoughts from afar.
~ Psalm 139:2 NIV ~

May 9

You Know Everything about Me

"For God so loved the world that He gave His only Son, so that everyone who believes in Him will not perish but have eternal life."
~ *John 3:16* ~

Father, I would have to admit that one of the most amazing things I have to consider is how You know me so well and yet love me anyway. Your love does not depend on my strengths and weaknesses, or my successes or failures. Your love does not step back when I do foolish things or diminish when I forget to say I love You in return.

You know everything about me and You continue to love me for the sake of Your Son, Jesus. Lord, I can hardly wrap my arms around that. I fall down and You lift me up. I shake my puny fist in anger and You come closer to protect my heart and mind.

I will always be awed by You. *Amen.*

You have searched me, LORD, and You know me.
~ *Psalm 139:1* NIV ~

In Praise of Get-togethers!

For you have been called to live in freedom. But don't use your freedom to satisfy your sinful nature. Instead, use your freedom to serve one another in love.
~ Galatians 5:13 ~

Lord, I love those friendly get-togethers with people who share the blessings of living in Your name.

I pray today that You would continue to gather Your flocks together, so they might encourage each other. I pray for those who feel isolated or shut-in, who do not have the choice or the chance to get together with like-minded souls. Be there to comfort them and remind them of Your glorious presence.

Bless those who are willing to extend the hand of fellowship. Remind us of the incredible luxury and freedom we have to come together any time we want to worship You. *Amen.*

And you shall gather yourselves together frequently, seeking what is fitting for your souls.
~ Didache ~

May 11

Season of Joy!

The winter is past, and the rains are over and gone. The flowers are springing up, the season of singing birds has come.

~ Song of Songs 2:11-12 ~

Dear Lord, I thank You that You have found so many ways to help me feel strong and happy. You've given me seasons of growth and renewal. You've kept me safe, always holding the promise of the possibility of what is to come.

I thank You for giving me blessings beyond measure. As the springtime blossoms bring new fragrance to the air, let my joy also bloom and grow in Your care and keeping.

Help me remember in those moments when life is difficult, to hold on to the bigger picture, the greater opportunity that comes from knowing You. Thank You that even my happiness is important to You. *Amen.*

Bring joy to Your servant,
Lord, for I put my trust in You.
~ Psalm 86:4 *NIV* ~

May Love Increase

And may the Lord make your love for one another and for all people grow and overflow, just as our love for you overflows.

~ 1 Thessalonians 3:12 ~

Lord, I know I'm no different than anyone else. I talk a good game about loving my neighbor, but I'm not always the first one there when help is needed.

I ask today that You would help me to see my friends and neighbors as You see them. Help me to see their hearts first and to be more careful about judging their actions. Help me to want to know the truth before I start sharing stories that come to me from third parties, stories that I don't know for sure have any credibility. Help me not to undermine another one of Your children in any way.

Teach me to love people and to increase my desire to love them in everything I do. *Amen.*

Your love, Lord, reaches to the heavens,
Your faithfulness to the skies.
~ Psalm 36:5 *NIV* ~

Motivational Moment

People may be right in their own eyes, but the Lord examines their heart.

~ Proverbs 21:2 ~

Lord, help me understand the best way to align my heart with Yours so that I might engage in the right work at the right time. Motivate my spirit in such a way that it cannot rest until it begins the work in earnest that You have called me to do.

When I feel overwhelmed with a sense of urgency, but no sense of direction, I simply stand still. I do not seem to accomplish anything that would be considered worthwhile. It is my heart's desire to please You and to fulfill my purpose. This is not something I can manage on my own.

Please be with me and all those who seek Your guidance as they strive to move forward with their life's mission. Help me to begin again and then bless the path I take. *Amen.*

For the Lord watches over the way of the righteous.

~ Psalm 1:6 NIV ~

May 14

Open My Eyes

"Your eye is a lamp that provides light for your body. When your eye is good, your whole body is filled with light."

~ Matthew 6:22 ~

Father, I know that my eyes are dim. I do not see all that You have put before me. I am not fully aware of Your presence and Your love for me.

Open my eyes and help me to see You, more fully, more reverently. Fill my body with the light of Your Spirit in ways that would illuminate my path and bring me to the places You'd have me be.

I ask for my soul to be awash with the sunshine of Your love and power. May I stand in Your light so that I can better share that light with others.

Forgive me for walking in darkness, when You have been so generous as to give me the light of Your Son. Help me to see You more clearly with a bright, clean heart. *Amen.*

I lie down and sleep; I wake again,
because the LORD sustains me.

~ Psalm 3:5 *NIV* ~

Prayers for Preachers

Preach the word of God. Be prepared, whether the time is favorable or not. Patiently correct, rebuke, and encourage your people with good teaching.
~ 2 Timothy 4:2 ~

Lord, I want to lift up all those men and women who speak for You in this world.

Wherever and whenever someone rises to speak of You, to preach Your Gospel of grace, I pray that they might be truly anointed by You. I pray, Lord, that they would have a heart for You like none other and that their whole motivation would be to express Your love and Your salvation plan for Your children.

We live at a time in history when people struggle to know You, are eager to hear about You, and are ready to receive You. Bless those who preach and teach and strive to bring hope to them all. *Amen.*

Many, Lord, are asking, "Who will bring us prosperity?" Let the light of Your face shine on us.
~ Psalm 4:6 *NIV* ~

May 16

Just Press On!

We are pressed on every side by troubles, but we are not crushed. We are hunted down, but never abandoned by God.

~ *2 Corinthians 4:8-9* ~

Lord, I'm not a quitter! Sometimes I feel defeated and I wonder if the desires of my heart will actually come to fruition, but I won't quit. You gave me these desires, You set my life in motion and prepared a particular path for me to walk and so I look to You now to help me walk that path.

Help me to not look so long at the obstacles and the troubles that I miss the triumphs. Let me embrace those who would help me move forward and give me the opportunity to succeed. Whenever I get knocked down, Father, I ask that You would raise me up again to fight another day.

Bless all those who struggle with some kind of trial today and be their Champion. *Amen.*

From the LORD comes deliverance.
May Your blessing be on Your people.
~ *Psalm 3:8 NIV* ~

Having the Time of Your Life

"That is why I tell you not to worry about everyday life – whether you have enough food and drink, or enough clothes to wear. Isn't life more than food, and your body more than clothing?"

~ Matthew 6:25 ~

Lord, sometimes I think so much about the future, that I position everything as "life will be better when …" and so I miss the present.

Help me remember today that this is the day that I have. This is the moment for me to have the time of my life, because it is truly the only time I have.

Bless all of us who strive to live a life that is pleasing to You and worthy of Your grace. Help us to let go of our worries, cease to struggle over the future, at least for a little while, and rest in Your loving arms today. *Amen.*

The Lord has done it this very day;
let us rejoice today and be glad.
~ Psalm 118:24 NIV ~

May 18

I'll Be the Judge of That!

The first to speak in court sounds right – until the cross-examination begins.
~ Proverbs 18:17 ~

Father, forgive me when I make hasty judgments about another person. Sometimes with no information at all, I assume I know their story and worse yet, that I could share their story with someone else. The fact is, I don't know their story or I probably only know a thread of their story and it's been woven by so many hands, I have no clear idea of the truth.

I know that I do not like people making snap judgments about me. I want only You to judge me according to my worth in the eyes of Jesus. Help me remember that wherever I go so that I see everyone as an extension of Your love.

I ask Your forgiveness for each time I set myself up to be the judge of someone else. Replace judgment with truth and understanding. *Amen.*

I have hidden Your word in my heart
that I might not sin against You.
~ Psalm 119:11 NIV ~

The Wisdom of Age

Those who are older should speak, for wisdom comes with age.

~ Job 32:7 ~

Lord of my heart, help me to be wise. I've always hoped there would be truth in the idea that wisdom comes with age. Certainly life experience helps us to make new choices or to try again when we fail. We learn from our mistakes, even when we have to make the same mistake again.

Grant that I may shine Your light with truth and wisdom no matter what my age. Help me to be a guardian of Your will and Your desires for human-kind. Help me to speak up and stand up for You when a situation demands that I do so.

I pray for all Your people who seek to know more of You and to be wiser in the ways they live and work. I ask for Your blessing today and always.

Amen.

It is the province of knowledge to speak
and it is the privilege of wisdom to listen.
~ Oliver Wendell Holmes ~

May 20

Reinventing Yourself

This means that anyone who belongs to Christ has become a new person. The old life is gone; a new life has begun!

~ 2 Corinthians 5:17 ~

Lord, here I am, reinventing myself again! It seems like I've started down a hundred different paths only to find myself right back here, standing in front of You. I seek Your guidance as I move on with my life, Your wisdom for each step I take.

Help me become the kind of person who sees Your hand at work in everyone I meet. When I do that, I'm more willing to be patient and to seek to learn from them.

I pray for all of Your people who want to change, who want to become more of what You designed them to be. Help them, and help me to be ready to hear Your voice and to act on Your command. *Amen.*

Have mercy on me, O God, according to Your unfailing love; according to Your great compassion blot out my transgressions.

~ Psalm 51:1 NIV ~

Busy as a Bee

Work willingly at whatever you do, as though you were working for the Lord rather than for people.
~ Colossians 3:23 ~

Lord, I have a heavy load of work in front of me. I'll be as busy as a bee trying to get it all done. Please help me to not neglect our relationship in the midst of my own busyness. Help me to remember to start my work with Your blessing and guidance and to end my work with a grateful heart.

Bless my busyness so that it matters to my life and the lives of those around me. Help the work of my hands to flourish and grow according to Your plans set down before I ever arrived on this planet.

Let me be glad-hearted about all that I do so that the light of Your spirit shines through my work. Whether I'm working at home or an office or simply to become a better person, help me to always work for You. *Amen.*

God is a busy worker, but loves to be helped.
~ Proverb ~

Making Things Grow

*It's not important who does the planting, or who does
the watering. What's important is that God makes the
seed grow.*

~ 1 Corinthians 3:7 ~

Lord, thank You for providing all that I need to help
me grow. Thank You for my home which nourishes
my roots and provides for my well-being. It is here
that I experience the values I've come to know and
which offer me a stable environment.

Thank You for teachers and pastors and those
who guide my spiritual growth so that I can grow in
my faith to a place that is worthy and strong. Thank
You for putting just the right people in my path with
a word of encouragement or caution or who offer
prayers on my behalf.

I ask that You would continue to help me grow, to
find my place in the world and yet to be rooted fully
in Your love and grace. *Amen.*

*The righteous will flourish like a palm tree, they will grow
like a cedar of Lebanon; planted in the house of the LORD.*

~ Psalm 92:12-13 *NIV* ~

May 23

Making a Good Choice

Today I have given you the choice between life and death, between blessings and curses. Now I call on heaven and earth to witness the choice you make.

~ Deuteronomy 30:19 ~

Lord, I am more than aware that I have often made choices that did not serve me well. I know that I have disappointed You many times.

I pray now that You would forgive me for those bad choices and guide me towards the things that are best for me. Help me to desire more of the good things that come only from You and please be the One who shapes and molds me.

I know that even when I fall short of the mark, in my heart, I always choose You. I choose You to be my Lord and my Savior. I choose You to be the guide and guardian of my spirit. I ask for Your help in choosing wisely in all that I do. *Amen.*

The LORD watches over you – the LORD is your shade at your right hand; the sun will not harm you by day, nor the moon by night.

~ Psalm 121:5-6 *NIV* ~

May 24

Faith for Tomorrow

Don't brag about tomorrow, since you don't know what the day will bring.
~ Proverbs 27:1 ~

Father, it seems like I spend a lot more time worrying about tomorrow than I do about just living today. Those who like to predict what they believe may come in the future, do it with gusto, giving all of us pause to wonder if we should take it in.

Yet, the fact remains that You are in control. Only You know whether tomorrow will indeed arrive. Only You hold the future in Your hand.

Help me, Lord, to not fear the days ahead and spend time puzzling over what may or may not be. Help me, instead, to embrace today with such fervor that I can't help but make something useful out of it.

Be with me, I pray, and give me the strength to continue to plant seeds for the future, but to live on the fruit of all that I have for today. *Amen.*

May you live to see your children's children.
~ Psalm 128:6 NIV ~

A Little Happy Dance

For the happy heart, life is a continual feast.
~ *Proverbs 15:15* ~

Dear Lord, my heart is happy today. It's happy any time I stop to look at all the treasures You've given me. I have an incredible abundance because of Your love. For what material possession could ever take the place of knowing I'm free to communicate with You at any given moment?

What title of respect as this world claims titles, could possibly give me more hope and possibility than the one You gave me when You called me Your child and Your friend?

You are my heart, Lord, my true treasure and so I pray today that You would always stay close to me and that You would bless the people all over the planet who keep their hearts closely aligned with Yours. In Jesus' name, I ask this. *Amen.*

Exult in His holy name; rejoice,
you who worship the LORD.
~ *Psalm 105:3 NIV* ~

Death, Be Not Proud

*The wicked are crushed by disaster, but the godly have
a refuge when they die.*

~ Proverbs 14:32 ~

Father, I suspect that I'm as fearful as anyone when it comes to thinking about death, and yet, as John Donne so aptly put it, death is not truly the end of life. Perhaps it is only the beginning. Perhaps after we attend this earth school, we find a new world opens up and an amazing life begins.

I pray for those near me who have recently passed away. I ask that You receive them all with open arms of love and mercy. I pray for those who suffer the loss of someone they love, that they may find hope in knowing that death does not have the last word.

Thank You for loving us so much, that You provide comfort for our souls in matters of life, and of death. *Amen.*

*The LORD has dealt with me according
to my righteousness; according to the
cleanness of my hands He has rewarded me.*

~ Psalm 18:20 NIV ~

Because Life Goes On

"For it is My Father's will that all who see His Son and believe in Him should have eternal life. I will raise them up at the last day."

~ *John 6:40* ~

Father, I am so grateful that life goes on. This brief span of time that we exist on earth only gives us a taste of what life can be. Lord, I pray for my brothers and sisters everywhere that each one of them would come to know You while they are still in the body, so they may rejoice with You once they are only in the spirit.

Help us to desire more of You and to realize that we only have a little bit of time to choose where we want to go from here. Help us to embrace You so that the dance of life for now and from here is more blessed. Help us to take whatever steps are necessary to walk closer to You. *Amen.*

Surely Your goodness and love will follow me all the days of my life, and I will dwell in the house of the Lord forever.

~ *Psalm 23:6* NIV ~

A Golden Nugget

Humbly accept the word God has planted in your hearts, for it has the power to save your souls.
~ James 1:21 ~

Lord, You have given me so many ways to understand what You want from me. You've given me Your Word so that I may have a constant guide when life overwhelms me and uncertainty comes. You've given me good friends to help keep me strong in the midst of obstacles and pain.

You've also given me golden nuggets of advice that I may live wisely and well. You've taught me that the more I'm willing to follow Your ways, the more I see a clear path before me.

Help me to obey You in matters of my life and heart, help me to turn to You when I am fearful or uncertain of my direction. Help me to understand that You always work in my life for my good and that You are truly a loving Father to me. *Amen.*

Blessed are all who fear the LORD,
who walk in obedience to Him.
~ Psalm 128:1 *NIV* ~

All but for a
Little Patience

Be patient with everyone.
~ 1 Thessalonians 5:14 ~

Lord, I have not been the most patient of people. I ask that You would teach me the kind of loving, ever-faithful, steadfast patience that You have.

Help me to be less sensitive to those little things that certainly don't matter at the end of the day … the person who got ahead of me in line, or the one who pulled into the parking spot I was waiting patiently to enter. I know that You call us to be patient with everyone, because we cannot possibly know everyone else's story. We cannot know what motivates them, or what causes them to be as they are.

Lord, grant me a better attitude about all those little disturbances that cause me to lose my patience. Help me in this way to be more like You. *Amen.*

I wait for the LORD, my whole being waits,
and in His word I put my hope.
~ Psalm 130:5 NIV ~

May 30

Praise and Thanks!

Sing to the Lord, for He has done wonderful things.
Make known His praise around the world.
~ Isaiah 12:5 ~

Lord, I know I am so remiss in the area of praise. I know that I have not begun to thank You for all You've done in providing for Your children here on earth and for providing for me in particular.

Forgive me and accept my heartfelt thanks and praise. There is no God but You, no Creator of the universe, but You. You are the true light of the world and without You all of earth would be cast into utter darkness.

Father, I thank You for Your protection, Your kindness, Your mercy and forgiveness. I thank You that even knowing the hearts of humankind, even knowing how often we sin against You, that You continue to love us.

Help me to be worthy of Your love. *Amen.*

I will extol the Lord at all times; His praise will
always be on my lips. I will glory in the Lord.
~ Psalm 34:1-2 NIV ~

I rise today with the power of God to guide me,
the might of God to uphold me,
the wisdom of God to teach me,
the eye of God to watch over me,
the ear of God to hear me,
the word of God to give me speech,
the hand of God to protect me,
the path of God to lie before me,
the shield of God to shelter me,
the host of God to defend me
against the snares of the devil
and the temptations of the world,
against every man who meditates injury to me,
whether far or near.
Amen.

~ Prayer of St. Patrick ~

June

Possibility Thinking

Is anything too hard for the LORD?
~ Genesis 18:14 ~

Dear Lord, I have a heart today for all those who aren't exactly where they hoped they'd be by now and regret some of the choices they've made. I also want to pray for those who have lost their way and can't see that You still have hope and a future to offer them.

I've been there, too. I've spent too much time regretting past decisions and wondering about the "what-if's" of life. Lord, I know that with You everything is possible. You are the One who can help us open new windows and walk through new doors. I pray that You would help all of us who are stuck in some way today. *Amen.*

When one door closes another door opens;
but we so often look so long and so regretfully
upon the closed door, that we do not see
the ones which open before us.
~ Alexander Graham Bell ~

Narrow Escapes

I have been reduced to skin and bones and have escaped death by the skin of my teeth.

~ Job 19:20 ~

Lord, I know I need to give all thanks and praise to You that I have escaped miseries that I'm not even aware could have been. Your grace and mercy have kept me from making choices that would not have been good for me.

Lord, I thank You for causing me to escape those places that would harm my spirit or my body. I thank You for protecting me even from myself when I do not recognize a place of danger.

Bless all those today, who face some kind of potential threat to their well-being and provide an escape – whether they are driving a car, walking in a dangerous neighborhood, or simply contemplating an act that would not serve them or You. I ask You this in Jesus' name. *Amen.*

If we escape one error,
we usually glide into its opposite.
~ Charles H. Spurgeon ~

I Can Do It!

The time has come and I won't hold back; I will not change my mind.

~ Ezekiel 24:14 ~

Lord, I ask that You would be with me today as I begin again to take the path You have directed. Help me to be determined and focused. Help me to persevere and win the day. I know with Your help I can do it!

When my spirit is pumped up and ready to act, I feel so excited and the world can hardly contain my hopes and possibility. Then, some little setback comes along and I start to doubt, start to wonder if I'm doing the right thing after all.

Please be with me when I question myself and keep me clear about the choices I make. Bless all those who seek Your affirmation. The time has indeed come, Lord, for Your children to win at the missions You have given to each of them. Bless each one!

Amen.

O LORD, save us; O LORD, grant us success.

~ Psalm 118:25 NIV ~

Family Matters

God Himself has taught you to love one another.
~ 1 Thessalonians 4:9 ~

Lord, You placed us in families so we could get a taste of love and understand how to live together. Our families gave us breadth and depth of character and helped us make good choices. Ideally, our families helped us learn what it means to love one another as You have commanded.

Today, I pray for all families everywhere across the world. I pray for parents who truly love their children as You love their children. I pray for wisdom and patience and forgiveness for those who guide the hearts and minds of others. I pray for strength for families that are falling apart.

I thank You too for my own family, for in Your wisdom, I was placed in their care and given the opportunity to become all that I am today. Bless my family with Your love and grace and mercy! Bless all families. *Amen.*

God sets the lonely in families.
~ Psalm 68:6 NIV ~

June 4

Wandering Hearts

So I said to myself, "I will get up now and roam the city, searching for him in all its streets and squares." But my search was in vain.

~ Song of Songs 3:2 ~

Lord, I feel a bit like a wanderer on this great planet. I feel like I've been searching for something, something I cannot quite describe. Perhaps in some way that I have not yet imagined, I've been searching for You, the God of my heart.

Often, I receive glimpses of You, the feeling that You are very near and very present. I see You come through the smile of a stranger or the momentary encounter with someone on the street.

You are present and real and so I know the search is not in vain. I know that I am not lost at all, but have already been found and redeemed by You. I pray for all who wander, all who seek more of You, that You would give them the satisfaction of feeling Your arms around them today. *Amen.*

Not all those who wander are lost.

~ J. R. R. Tolkien ~

Seeking Your Voice

"I have spoken to you again and again, and you refuse to listen or obey."

~ Jeremiah 35:14 ~

Lord, help me to listen when You speak. How many times do I offer up my prayers to You and then forget to wait, to listen, to see what You might share with me then and there? The noise in the world overwhelms me sometimes. I cannot always find respite from the information that comes pouring in through every electronic device known to humankind. Once I was hungry for information, like everyone else.

Now I hunger more for You, for the quiet connection that only You can bring through a means that is far more powerful than the internet. Help me to screen out the cacophony and seek only Your voice. Bless all who want more of You and less of the world.

Amen.

Give ear to my words, O LORD, consider my sighing. Listen to my cry for help, my King and my God, for to You I pray.

~ Psalm 5:1-2 NIV ~

June 6

Miracle Moments

"Teacher," he said, "we all know that God has sent You to teach us. Your miraculous signs are proof enough that God is with You."

~ John 3:2 ~

Lord, I have friends who don't think You're in the miracle business any more, and yet, everything I see around me, feels miraculous.

The fact is, You created gravity so I don't think You can actually defy anything. You simply change the direction of something You started anyway.

I thank You for anything that helps people see You, believe You and want more of You. I thank You for miracles that help others discover how incredible You are! *Amen.*

At strategic moments God again and again manifested Himself to men by miracles so they had outward, confirming evidence that the words they heard from God's servants were true.

~ Billy Graham ~

Giving and Getting

You must each make up your own mind as to how much you should give. Don't give reluctantly or in response to pressure. For God loves the person who gives cheerfully.

~ 2 Corinthians 9:7 ~

Lord, sometimes I feel so overwhelmed by the hundreds of charities, churches, and organizations that ask for donations. Most of the time, I am scarcely keeping up with my own bills and responsibilities and I lose sight of how to be a cheerful giver.

I do my best to give my time, my heart, and my conversations to people who are near me. I offer encouragement and compassion and kindness. Lord, I pray, too, for those people who have abundance and can give easily and freely. Help them to be aware that giving is more than just a financial arrangement. That giving and getting are always matters of the heart. *Amen.*

Blessed are those who give without remembering and take without forgetting.
~ Elizabeth Bibesco ~

A Humble Experience

So humble yourselves before God. Resist the devil, and he will flee from you. Draw close to God, and God will draw close to you.

~ James 4:7-8 ~

Lord, I am indeed humbled by my own willingness to be deceived, to lie to myself about things that I do that are not serving You or me well. I am humbled each time I must acknowledge that I do not do everything right. Help me to resist the devil, those things that would seek to deprive me of a closer walk with You.

Forgive me once again, Lord, for losing my way and let it be for me an experience of deep humility. Thank You for loving me so much that You seek always my highest good, even when You have to bring me to my knees to do that. *Amen.*

The LORD is close to the brokenhearted and saves those who are crushed in spirit.

~ Psalm 34:18 *NIV* ~

An Abundant Life

"The thief's purpose is to steal and kill and destroy.
My purpose is to give life in all its fullness."
~ *John 10:10* ~

Lord, I confess that I've often gotten it wrong when I tried to imagine what it meant to have an abundant life. I used to think it meant that I'd never have a financial care, that I'd be able to do whatever I wanted, enjoy good health and see my children become strong and happy adults.

I used to think that abundance had something to do with material possessions and things that I could count or number.

Abundance in this life comes from one thing. It comes from knowing that You are the Source of all that is good, that You are the sustainer, provider, and deliverer. I have an abundant life, Father. Because of You, I have all I will ever need. *Amen.*

The earth is the Lord's and everything in it, the world,
and all who live in it; for He founded it upon the seas
and established it upon the waters.
~ *Psalm 24:1-2 NIV* ~

But, It Isn't Fair!

The LORD despises those who acquit the guilty and condemn the innocent.

~ Proverbs 17:15 ~

Dear Lord, it helps to know that You despise those times when the guilty go free and the innocent are persecuted. Of course, You know how that feels because it is exactly what happened when Your innocent Son was sent to die.

Help us pursue the goal of justice for all people everywhere. It isn't easy and even in our own lives, even in my life, I recognize those times when life just isn't fair.

I pray for all people who need Your justice. I pray today for You to always be in control and help us create a more just world for each other. *Amen.*

Justice and power must be brought together,
so that whatever is just may be powerful, and whatever
is powerful may be just.

~ Blaise Pascal ~

A Little Compassion

"Do for others what you would like them to do for you. This is a summary of all that is taught in the law and the prophets."

~ Matthew 7:12 ~

Father, bless those who need more kindness and compassion. Help me to see ways to offer light into the day of anyone who may be struggling, suffering in a personal darkness. Help me to see Your face on a stranger and seek Your heart in a friend.

Help me to be patient with those who are difficult, who have a different temperament from mine and need me to slow down or speed up to walk with them. Remind me how important it is for me to be all I can to each person I meet, to represent You in any way possible. Bless all of us, Lord, and help us be more compassionate. *Amen.*

The LORD is gracious and compassionate,
slow to anger and rich in love.
~ Psalm 145:8 NIV ~

Slings and Arrows

"Stop judging others, and you will not be judged."
~ Matthew 7:1 ~

Lord, I ask Your forgiveness for those times when I've made snap judgments about people, assuming I knew their motives, their stories.

I ask forgiveness because I don't like it when this happens to me. So many times, I've suffered the opinion of someone hoping to "set me straight" only to realize that they know nothing of me really, nothing of my relationship with You and why I act as I do.

All of us suffer the slings and arrows that others send our way, some times hitting the mark in a way that brings us great pain. Help us to forgive as quickly as possible when those things happen so that we can move on in an effort to grow closer to You. *Amen.*

Criticism, like rain, should be gentle enough to nourish a man's growth without destroying his roots.
~ Frank A. Clark ~

June 13

Free as the Wind

"You will know the truth, and the truth will set you free."

~ John 8:32 ~

Lord, thank You that I am free to worship You. Thank You that I can live and breathe and have my being in Your Spirit. Your love and Your truth have set me free.

I ask Your healing on those who are still trapped in the darkness, still wandering about in a state of uncertainty, roaming the planet with no place to go. I ask that You would turn up the light for them to see You more clearly and set their hearts free to love You and serve You. I ask this, Father, because of Your beloved Son who truly set us all free. *Amen.*

Long my imprisoned spirit lay,
Fast bound in sin and nature's night;
Thine eye diffused a quickening ray
I woke, the dungeon flamed with light.
My chains fell off, my heart was free
I rose, went forth, and followed Thee.
~ Charles Wesley ~

June 14

Powerful Prayers

*Remember, O my God, all that I have done for these
people, and bless me for it.*
~ Nehemiah 5:19 ~

Lord, I thank You for those who believe in the power
of prayer. I thank You for the example of ancient
prayer warriors and those that exist in our current
day. Nehemiah knew the work he had done for You
and prayed for Your blessing.

Whether we are aware of the work we do for You,
or whether we let Your light shine in a quieter way, I
ask for Your blessing.

I believe in prayer. I believe that through this awesome form of communication, You bring us closer to
Yourself and open the gates wider for more blessings
to come in. Thank You for loving us so much. *Amen.*

*None can believe how powerful prayer is,
and what it is able to effect, but those
who have learned it by experience.*
~ Martin Luther ~

This Way and That

Then Elijah stood in front of them and said, "How long are you going to waver between two opinions? If the LORD is God, follow Him! But if Baal is God, then follow him!" But the people were completely silent.
~ 1 Kings 18:21 ~

Lord, I like to think I'm not stubborn when it comes to my faith in You. I like to think that if Elijah stood in front of me, I could answer with a loud shout of affirmation that You are the Lord.

I wonder how many times I've been silent when an opportunity to witness my faith came up, or when I had to make a choice to do something that I wasn't quite sure You'd be happy about.

I ask Your forgiveness for those times, for keeping my faith like some kind of secret, instead of sharing it with the joy I have in You. I pray for all the people of faith that we would be strong and willing to declare our faith in You at all times. *Amen.*

Blessed are all who fear the LORD,
who walk in His ways.
~ Psalm 128:1 NIV ~

Facing Inward

Though our bodies are dying, our spirits are being renewed every day.

~ 2 Corinthians 4:16 ~

Lord, help me be more willing to look within myself for the place that connects me with You. Help me to desire more of You so that every outward act is one that brings joy to my soul and causes You to be proud of me.

It isn't always easy to maintain the kind of perspective that realizes how important our time together is for each of us. When I let the world in too much, I lose sight of what I have. When I return to You, return to the space where I pray more and sit closely by Your side, everything changes.

Father, I pray for all the believers who seek to be more closely connected to Your Spirit, that they may take the time to look within themselves. *Amen.*

The inward area is the first place of loss of true Christian life, of true spirituality, and the outward sinful act is the result.
~ Francis A. Schaeffer ~

Heaven Help Us!

But we are citizens of heaven, where the Lord Jesus Christ lives. And we are eagerly waiting for Him to return as our Savior.

~ *Philippians 3:20* ~

Gracious and Most Loving God, it is with great awe that I consider the idea of heaven, a place where there is no suffering, no sorrow, no heartache. It brings such hope to weary souls simply to contemplate the goodness and joy of heaven.

Lord, I pray for all Your children. I pray for those who know You well. I pray for those who aren't quite sure yet about their connection to You. I pray that You would strengthen that connection, strengthen their desire to be closer to You. I pray too for those who do not yet know You, who walk sleepy-eyed in a kind of strange darkness. Yes, I pray for them most fervently. Bless all Your children so that they might one day come home again to You. *Amen.*

The main object of religion is not to get a man into heaven, but to get heaven into him.
~ *Thomas Hardy* ~

June 18

Just the Clay

And yet, LORD, You are our Father. We are the clay, and You are the Potter. We are all formed by Your hand.

~ Isaiah 64:8 ~

Lord, help me to simply be the clay, ready any time to be remolded and reshaped. I know out of one piece of clay, You can create hundreds of opportunities for service, a myriad of options for potential uses.

Remind me that You are indeed the Potter and I am the clay. Help me to let go of the old me any time You feel I need to be reshaped and made new. Help me to let go of yesterday and to embrace today, so that I can be a useful vessel right where I am.

I pray for all those You have shaped by Your hand and ask You to bless each one according to Your will and purpose. *Amen.*

I praise You because I am fearfully and wonderfully made; Your works are wonderful, I know that full well.
~ Psalm 139:14 NIV ~

Being Happily Content

I have learned how to get along happily whether I have much or little.

~ Philippians 4:11 ~

Lord, how often do I shake my puny fist at You, quibbling over one small matter after another? How often do I set my worries up like icons to be polished and enjoyed, rather than leaving them in Your powerful hand?

Help me to be content in all situations for when I am, I know that it means my heart is at rest in You. Be with all those who need to put their troubles to rest, and guide them to simply come closer to You. Help them to see that You offer them the gift of true peace no matter what life circumstances may look like.

Whether we have abundance, or we simply have enough, whether we're uncertain of tomorrow, or totally secure, let us find our true peace and security in You. *Amen.*

Blessed is the man who makes the LORD his trust.
~ Psalm 40:4 NIV ~

Just a Bit of Courage

Be strong with the Lord's mighty power.
~ Ephesians 6:10 ~

Lord, please grant that I might have more courage in my everyday life … the courage to stand up for what I believe, the courage to be myself, and the courage to love unconditionally. It is not always easy to be courageous when so many fearful things assault us on every side.

Lord, thank You for being in control of this world, for Your faithful blessings and gifts and Your enduring love. Grant the gift of courage to each person who seeks Your face. *Amen.*

Courage is the best gift of all; courage stands
before everything. It is what preserves our liberty, safety,
life, and our homes and parents, our
country and children. Courage comprises all
things: a person with courage has every blessing.
~ Plautus ~

Just Carry On!

Mark out a straight path for your feet; then stick to the path and stay safe.

~ Proverbs 4:26 ~

Lord, help me to align the direction of my life with the dreams You have for me, the ones You placed inside my heart before I was even born. Help me to achieve my life purpose, my mission of worth so that I might faithfully serve You. Be my light on the path I take as I go forward.

Sometimes it feels like I don't know where I'm going and so I pray also that You would walk with me all along the way. Put me on the path to somewhere … somewhere only You wanted me to go … somewhere You already assigned to me.

Help all of us who seek Your guidance to carry on with trust and joy knowing You are with us all the way. I ask Your blessing on all that I do today to further my direction and my dreams. *Amen.*

If you don't know where you are going,
every road will get you nowhere.
~ Henry Kissinger ~

June 22

Reach for a Star!

Remember that in a race everyone runs, but only one person gets the prize. You also must run in such a way that you will win.

~ 1 Corinthians 9:24 ~

Lord, I love to set new goals and challenge myself to meet their possibility. I'm glad that You made me a possibility thinker because it adds a dimension of quality to my life.

I know that I don't have to be a star for You to love me. I know I don't have to win every race for You to see me in a special way.

I pray that You would help me to keep seeking my best self. Help me to be willing to do the work to achieve my goals and to remember that You gave me every shred of skill and talent that I have to make those goals possible. Thank You for helping me reach for a star. *Amen.*

Becoming a star may not be your destiny,
but being the best that you can be is a
goal that you can set for yourself.
~ Bryan Lindsay ~

In Praise of Friends

As iron sharpens iron, a friend sharpens a friend.
~ Proverbs 27:17 ~

Lord, I can't thank You and praise You enough for my friends. I know that You have given each one of them to me to share something significant in my life. You've given me long-term friends who have shared my ups and downs and who have supported me through those moments that I simply could not bear to walk alone.

You have given me new friends who give me a chance to be myself, the one who enters into a relationship with joy and abandon.

I need both kinds of friends though and I'm thankful for the give and take of any of those relationships. Bless my friends today, Lord, with an extra measure of Your grace and mercy. *Amen.*

At times our own light goes out and is rekindled
by a spark from another person. Each of us has
cause to think with deep gratitude of those
who have lighted the flame within us.
~ Albert Schweitzer ~

The Gift of Little Things

We know that God causes everything to work together for the good of those who love God.
~ Romans 8:28 ~

Lord, as I look back over the years of my life, I marvel at the things that have made a difference, that have caused me to reconsider my path, or take another look at my own attitudes and behaviors. I realize that it was the kindness of a stranger that often made a day special or the close conversation with a sibling. Most of the time, it was a moment shared with someone who seemed to receive me just as I am and who lifted me up with a little gift of understanding and compassion.

Lord, bless all those people who offer a helping hand or an encouraging word, people who make a difference in the lives of others simply by doing little things with big hearts. *Amen.*

It is only in fidelity in little things that
a true and constant love of God can be
distinguished from a passing fervor of spirit.
~ François Fénelon ~

June 25

To See Things Clearly

Only the wise can give good advice.
~ Proverbs 15:7 ~

Lord, grant me the gifts of wisdom and discernment. Let me see clearly through the windows that open to new opportunities, to the people that come into my life and to the steps I take in my work. Help me to desire to know Your plans for me, to be impressed with Your Spirit in such a way that I am more precise in the things I do.

I pray that all my decisions would be made with true discernment and continual prayer. Only You know what is best for me. Only You know what work I should do and what people to invite into my life. Help me to be willing to stop, to pray, to think and then finally to act according to Your will. *Amen.*

Faith is the divine evidence whereby the spiritual man discerns God, and the things of God.
~ John Wesley ~

A Daily Dose of You

God is love, and all who live in love live in God, and God lives in them. And as we live in God, our love grows more perfect.

~ 1 John 4:16-17 ~

Here I am, Lord, back again. It seems like I can't get by for long on my own. I depend on You, on the times we get together to be in each other's presence. I need Your guidance for the things I do in my work, for the things I do in my heart, and those things that affect my spirit. I need You all the time.

I pray that You would not ever let me get far from Your grasp, never wander too long on my own terms, because I know what happens then. I know that I'll find myself in a situation or a place that I don't want to be and I'll feel alone and lost there. Be with me, every day, Lord, and be with all those who call upon Your name. *Amen.*

How often do we need to see God's face, hear His voice, feel His touch, know His power? The answer to all these questions is the same: Every day!

~ John Blanchard ~

Who Cares?

Don't think only of your own good. Think of other Christians and what is best for them.
~ 1 Corinthians 10:24 ~

Lord, You gave us deep sensitivity toward each other. You gave us an awareness of other's needs and have taught us ways that we can be a blessing to each other. You have shown us how to care for others in the same ways that You care for us.

Wherever I may be today, keep me aware of those in need of my nurture and my care. Help me be willing to reach out in a way that might make some small difference to their well-being as our paths cross.

Help me always to be a person who cares and who is willing and able to show I care by the things I say and do. Let me not withdraw from those in need, but work harder to see You in their faces, and if I do not find You there, may they see You reflected in me.

Amen.

But You are a shield around me, O Lord;
You bestow glory on me and lift up my head.
~ Psalm 3:3 NIV ~

June 28

The Worldwide Neighborhood

Are we not all children of the same Father? Are we not all created by the same God?
~ Malachi 2:10 ~

Lord, how often have I prayed, "For God so loved the world, He gave His only Son ..." Why is it that I often miss the part about Your love for the "world"?

Father, forgive me, when I don't stop to pray for my neighbors worldwide. The Internet has helped to connect people from every race and culture together, giving us more opportunity to know each other and to care about each other.

Bless those who work to carve lasting relationships between brothers and sisters around the globe. I pray that You would continue to help us learn to love one other. *Amen.*

Therefore, you kings, be wise; be warned,
you rulers of the earth. Serve the LORD
with fear and rejoice with trembling.
~ Psalm 2:10-11 NIV ~

Celebrate!

Always be full of joy in the Lord. I say it again – rejoice!

~ Philippians 4:4 ~

Lord, what beauty You have given us! I am in awe as I look at the richness of the universe, the incredible diversity of plants and animals, the amazing nuances of colors that are part of each thing You created.

Help us to always thrill at the vastness of the starry heavens, the luminous beams of the moon, and the promise of rainbows. There is so much reason to celebrate life and to rejoice in You!

Thank You for people who love life, for friendships, and families and pets.

We have so much to celebrate that it would take a continual prayer of unending joy to declare it all before You. Praise You, Father, for all You have done for Your children. *Amen.*

There is not one blade of grass, there is no color in this world that is not intended to make us rejoice.

~ John Calvin ~

June 30

Lord, make me an instrument of Your peace.
Where there is hatred, let me sow love,
Where there is injury, pardon;
Where there is doubt, faith;
Where there is despair, hope;
Where there is darkness, light;
Where there is sadness, joy.
O divine Master, grant that I may not so much seek
To be consoled, as to console;
To be understood, as to understand;
To be loved, as to love;
For it is in giving that we receive;
It is in pardoning that we are pardoned;
It is in dying that we are born to eternal life.

~ St. Francis of Assisi ~

July

Getting to Know You

Jesus answered, "Since you don't know who I am, you don't know who My Father is. If you knew Me, then you would know My Father, too."

~ John 8:19 ~

Lord, I know that I'm a long way from actually understanding Your nature, Your essence, and Your supernatural self. My imagination tries to put You into a perspective that I can grasp, but I'm sure that I'm far from the mark.

I pray that I would do a better job of getting to know You. I pray that I may be more open to the leading of Your Spirit, and seek to truly understand Your ways and Your desires.

I want to know You as Father, Son, and Holy Spirit and though it overwhelms my heart and mind to do that, I'm not afraid. Bless me with the wisdom and the desire to have more of You in my life. *Amen.*

The Lord confides in those who fear Him;
He makes His covenant known to them.

~ Psalm 25:14 *NIV* ~

Whenever I Feel Afraid

"I am leaving you with a gift – peace of mind and heart. And the peace I give isn't like the peace the world gives. So don't be troubled or afraid."
~ John 14:27 ~

Lord, I call on Your name today to be with all who live in fear. Remember those who fear for their lives because of wars or malnutrition or illness. Help them know that whatever the circumstance might be, however bleak things may appear that You are indeed with them.

Be with those who have other fears too, Lord. Be with the person who fears his job may end, or her marriage may fall apart. Grant Your gift of peace to all troubled souls that they may rest in You, find courage in Your grip, and know that You are always there. Help each one master any fear that exists and embrace Your peace. *Amen.*

The LORD is my light and my salvation – whom shall I fear? The LORD is the stronghold of my life – of whom shall I be afraid?
~ Psalm 27:1 NIV ~

July 2

The Faith Factor

You do not believe me? If you want me to protect you, learn to believe what I say.
~ Isaiah 7:9 ~

Father, I feel certain that you have placed a portion of Yourself within each one of us; a nugget of divine truth. From this truth, we have the option to grasp its goodness and nurture its growth. We can encourage it simply by the things we say and do.

Each time we choose to believe You, each time we trust that seed of faith, something changes. Somehow we are more connected to You and more able to trust in others too.

I pray for more faith. I pray for the faith of those who seek You with all their hearts and minds. I pray that those who do not yet understand that the light of Your Spirit is already within them might seek You more earnestly.

I pray that those who believe in You would live in great joy because of Your name. *Amen.*

The fear of the LORD is pure, enduring forever.
~ Psalm 19:9 NIV ~

Being a Little Kinder

*God can always point to us as examples of the incredible
wealth of His favor and kindness toward us, as shown
in all He has done for us through Christ Jesus.*
~ Ephesians 2:7 ~

Lord, we just can't plant enough seeds of kindness.
Everywhere we go, there are people deprived too
long of simple kindnesses. We are the ambassadors
of goodwill and the ones who must dispense Your
care to others.

I pray, Lord, that You would show me the opportunities I have today to be kind to someone else. Show
me the tired parent doing their duties who simply
needs someone to smile and recognize their hard
work. Whatever it is, however small it may seem,
help me be willing to plant seeds of encouragement
today. I ask this in Jesus' name. *Amen.*

*From heaven the Lord looks down and sees all
mankind; from His dwelling place He watches
all who live on earth – He who forms the hearts
of all, who considers everything they do.*
~ Psalm 33:13-15 NIV ~

A Little Education

Teach your children to choose the right path, and when they are older, they will remain upon it.
~ Proverbs 22:6 ~

Father, sometimes we think having an education has to do with college degrees. Though that may be one aspect of education, what we really need is spiritual education. We need to be able to discern right from wrong. We need to know when the company we work for isn't being a good steward of its resources or of the planet. We need to recognize how to manage our own resources in ways that benefit others.

Help us as we train our children, to teach them more than basic math and reading skills. Help us to teach them everlasting life skills. Those are the ones we hope will keep them safe on the path, keep them growing and walking toward You. Bless all who educate others today. *Amen.*

A man who has never gone to school may steal from a freight car; but if he has a university education, he may steal the whole railroad.
~ Theodore Roosevelt ~

That Is So Tempting

Remember that the temptations that come into your life are no different from what others experience. And God is faithful. He will keep the temptation from becoming so strong that you can't stand up against it. When you are tempted, He will show you a way out so that you will not give in to it.

~ 1 Corinthians 10:13 ~

Lord, sometimes we brush temptation aside as a small thing. We can be tempted by simple things that have some power over us, but we need to be aware of those bigger temptations.

Help us to overcome the temptation to break our marriage vows, or the temptation to not provide the boss with a good day's work. Help us to be aware of the choices we make that would go against the things You would have us do. We face temptations every day. Please help us be strong, and when we're not strong, help us find Your way out. *Amen.*

Free me from the trap that is set for me,
for You are my refuge.
~ Psalm 31:4 NIV ~

July 6

Not Proud of My Pride

Pride leads to disgrace, but with humility comes wisdom.

~ *Proverbs 11:2* ~

Father, I ask Your forgiveness for any bits of pride that I might allow into my life. I pray that any arrogance which may even remotely set itself up in my heart, might be instantly destroyed.

I ask that You would protect Your children from sins of pride in their work, their wealth and even their faith. Let us always remember that we are totally in need of Your continual grace and mercy.

Watch over those who are dangerously teetering on the brink of prideful actions, that they may turn from their arrogance, and put all things in Your hand. Let us boast only of our love for You. *Amen.*

According to Christian teachers, the essential vice, the utmost evil, is Pride. Unchastity, anger, greed, drunkenness, and all that, are mere flea bites in comparison: it was through Pride that the devil became the devil: Pride leads to every other vice.

~ *C. S. Lewis* ~

When God
Hears Prayers

"I have heard your prayer and seen your tears. I will heal you."

~ 2 Kings 20:5 ~

Lord, I am still in awe over Your desire to connect with Your children. You hear our prayers and listen to our complaints. You walk beside us even when we don't acknowledge You.

Thank You for allowing us to come before You any time of day or night and know that You will answer. Thank You that You're never too busy to answer us. I pray with a humble heart today that You would continue to fan the flames of my hope in You and answer those prayers that are for my good and the good of others according to Your will and purpose. *Amen.*

Prayer is not designed to inform God, but to give man a sight of his misery; to humble his heart, to excite his desire, to inflame his faith, to animate his hope, to raise his soul from earth to heaven.

~ Adam Clarke ~

July 8

Just a Little More Love

*Let love be your highest goal, but also desire the special
abilities the Spirit gives.*
~ 1 Corinthians 14:1 ~

Lord, I'm going to set out today to intentionally love
others. I want that to be the goal and I ask Your help
in doing so. I know that it isn't as simple a task as it
might sound, in fact, it's a huge task. After all, I have
to love the people in my household. I have to love
the people I work with and honor their thoughts and
ideas. I have to love strangers and try to see Your
light shining within them. Above all of that, I have
to exhibit love everywhere I go.

Bless the people in my household and give them
many reasons to praise You today. Bless each person
I work with and give them an extra measure of Your
Spirit as they try to reach personal goals. Let this be a
day filled with love for everyone I meet. *Amen.*

Love is itself the fulfillment of all our works.
There is the goal; that is why we run: we run toward it,
and once we reach it, in it we shall find rest.
~ St. Augustine ~

Choose the Abundant Life Today!

So whoever has God's Son has life; whoever does not have His Son does not have life.
~ 1 John 5:12 ~

Lord, sometimes I'm reminded about how much I seek eternal life, but forget to live the life You've given me here on earth. I forget to refresh myself each morning with Your Spirit so that I have more energy and sense of purpose.

Help me today, to choose to live abundantly, to choose to live fully connected to Your Spirit so that I might live with all my might. Help me to believe and to trust in You, so that I can live and walk in Your strength, according to Your might.

Help me not to be afraid to live this life as a redeemed and beloved child of God. Bless my life in You, so that I may live in Your joy. *Amen.*

Teach us to number our days aright,
that we may gain a heart of wisdom.
~ Psalm 90:12 NIV ~

July 10

Good Intentions

When I want to do good, I don't. And when I try not to do wrong, I do it anyway.
~ Romans 7:19 ~

Father, I'm ashamed to admit that I so often fall short of the mark. I have the best intentions, even speaking them aloud or writing them down for the things I want to do in a better way. I believe sincerely that I will make the effort. But before I know it, I've totally given in and fallen down again.

I ask Your help with my good intentions. Create in me the kind of heart and spirit that can withstand the mild temptations of life. It's the little things that trip me up, not the big things. Those little things that would make me feel like a more honorable person, that leave me wondering why I can't achieve them.

Be with everyone today who battles the best of intentions, not yet succeeding when they know they want to try. Give us strength in You to do better. I ask this in Jesus' holy name. *Amen.*

If better were within, better would come out.
~ Thomas Fuller ~

A Little Older and (Hopefully) Wiser!

If you need wisdom – if you want to know what God wants you to do – ask Him, and He will gladly tell you. He will not resent your asking.
~ James 1:5 ~

Oh, Lord, I thought by now, I'd have a pretty good grasp of life. I thought I would know what You want of me and what direction I should take. I hoped that getting older would somehow make me wiser.

I know that time does not have any meaning for You, but in my earthly body I have no choice but to make the best of the time I have. Perhaps, that is one blessing of being finite, we have to live better and more wisely. Help me to know what pleases You. I ask You to bless all who seek You and grant them greater wisdom. *Amen.*

The law of the LORD is perfect, reviving the soul.
The statutes of the LORD are trustworthy,
making wise the simple.
~ Psalm 19:7 NIV ~

July 12

Bitter Fruit

Get rid of all bitterness, rage, anger, harsh words, and slander. Instead, be kind to each other, tenderhearted, forgiving one another, just as God through Christ has forgiven you.

~ Ephesians 4:31-32 *NIV* ~

Father, forgive any bitter spirit that lives within me. Forgive me when I behave in unkind ways, or when I allow passing thoughts that are unjust or malicious. I hate to admit that I even do those things, but I own the truth of my behavior.

Lord, heal those who live even now with bitterness in their spirits. Remove the anger and the guilt and the frustration that they experience and cleanse their hearts and minds. I pray that You lift the bitterness from the hearts of all those who seek Your light today. *Amen.*

Bitterness imprisons life; love releases it. Bitterness paralyzes life; love empowers it. Bitterness sours life; love sweetens it. Bitterness sickens life; love heals it. Bitterness blinds life; love anoints its eyes.

~ Harry Emerson Fosdick ~

What Shall We Believe?

"If you don't even believe Me when I tell you about things that happen here on earth, how can you possibly believe if I tell you what is going on in heaven?"
~ John 3:12 ~

Lord, I do believe. I believe that You alone are the Creator of this universe and that You hold all the power on earth and in heaven. Thank You for allowing me the gift of grace so that I can embrace You. Thank You for giving me Your good news!

Many people live in this world and still hunger for You. Help them, Father! Please open the hearts of those who have been stubbornly refusing You, to those who have been blind to Your light or deaf to Your call. In Your mercy and in Your steadfast love, let none of them be lost. *Amen.*

If you can only believe! If you will only believe!
Then nothing, nothing will be impossible for you!
That is the truth and the gospel, and it is
wonderful. It's the good news.
~ Adapted from Norman Vincent Peale ~

Here's a New Thought!

There must be a spiritual renewal of your thoughts and attitudes.

~ Ephesians 4:23 ~

Dear Lord, it feels like so many people are deceived by a spirit of depression and negative attitudes. So many people suffer miseries that never befall them, worrying about what might be and missing what really is. I ask today that You would free any of us who do not have the attitude that embraces Your Spirit.

Help us to have more positive thoughts about all the little things that happen in our lives. Help us to embrace the good things. Let us ponder Your goodness and see the victory we have over life because of You.

Let each person that looks to You today be encouraged and shift their attitudes toward Your desires for them. *Amen.*

The Lord reigns, let the earth be glad;
let the distant shores rejoice.
~ Psalm 97:1 NIV ~

July 15

Ambition Matters

"Your heavenly Father already knows all your needs, and He will give you all you need from day to day if you live for Him and make the Kingdom of God your primary concern."

~ *Matthew 6:32-33* ~

Lord, help me to make it my true ambition to live for You. Help me to seek Your light in everything I attempt to do whether I fail or succeed.

Sometimes Bible words and ideas circle around me like misty angels and yet I know they are true. I know that I need to first and above all else, live for You and enhance Your Kingdom's work.

Open the doors for all who have an ambition to know more of You, who earnestly and whole-heartedly seek Your Kingdom and the ways to live within it on this earth. Let our ambitions matter to the heart and the soul. Let us achieve all things according to Your will and purpose for us. *Amen.*

I'd rather attempt something great and fail than to attempt nothing and succeed.
~ *Dr Robert H. Schuller* ~

Alone or Lonely?

My relatives stay far away, and my friends have turned against me. My neighbors and my close friends are all gone.

~ Job 19:13-14 ~

It is a wonder, Father, that any of us survive that bitter sense of loneliness. In that place where no one seems to validate You, where no one reaches out to offer comfort, life becomes painful.

Father, I pray today for all who suffer at the icy fingertips of loneliness. In its grasp is an utter feeling of being abandoned and left empty.

For the moments in my own life, when loneliness has washed over me like an unwelcome tide dragging me beneath its murky waters, I pray.

Be with us, Lord, and touch our lives in such a way that we know for certain that You are always near and we are always loved. *Amen.*

Loneliness and the feeling of being unwanted is the most terrible poverty.

~ Mother Teresa ~

July 17

Equal Opportunity

"He gives His sunlight to both the evil and the good,
and He sends rain on the just and on the unjust, too."
~ *Matthew 5:45* ~

Lord, I used to wonder why You would give every-thing good to those who do evil, just as much as You do good things for those who follow Your ways. I have to confess that there are times I wonder at why Your children suffer so badly in this world, while those who are not Your children seem to prosper.

As a good Father, You cannot but give good things and love everyone. Those who suffer in this life will surely walk with You in the next. Those who prosper without knowing You may not have the luxury of Your presence when this life is over.

I pray that I would be worthy to walk in Your presence in the world after this one. Help me to do good for all people wherever I am. *Amen.*

For the LORD is good and His love endures forever;
His faithfulness continues through all generations.
~ *Psalm 100:5 NIV* ~

Faithful Friends

Inside the Tent of Meeting, the Lord would speak to Moses face to face, as a man speaks to his friend.
~ Exodus 33:11 ~

Father in heaven, I ask today that You would lavish Your love on my friends. Lift up those who are concerned in any way about their health or their livelihood. Forgive those who have transgressions to put before You. Offer hope to those who are fearful or lost and seeking guidance to keep them on the right track.

I thank You for the people I am pleased to call my friends. I'm grateful to each one of them for the part they play in making a difference in life. I thank You for the laughter and the tears we share together.

Lord, bless my friends with abundant joy, and keep their hearts and minds close to You as well. May You also call each of them Your friend. *Amen.*

Of all the things which wisdom provides
to make us entirely happy, much the greatest
is the possession of friendship.
~ Epicurus ~

Defining Moments

"I see four men, unbound, walking around in the fire.
They aren't even hurt by the flames! And the fourth
looks like a divine being!"
~ Daniel 3:25 ~

God of my heart, I am awed by Your righteous power.
I am spellbound by the stories of those who have had
great faith and have learned to trust You so well. I
wonder what my faith would have done for me, had
I been cast in a fiery furnace. You send Your angels
into our midst at defining moments to give us a
glimpse of what is possible.

I pray for the defining moments in my own life.
I pray that I would have the strength to respond to
any situation with total trust in You. I pray for the
kind of faith that moves mountains. Help me to bind
up my doubts and leave all that I am, all that I can be,
totally in Your hands. I ask for the protection of Your
angels and the blessing of Your power and mercy in
all that I do. *Amen.*

I call on the LORD in my distress, and He answers me.
~ Psalm 120:1 *NIV* ~

July 20

Another Wrong Turn!

Don't copy the behavior and customs of this world, but let God transform you into a new person by changing the way you think.

~ Romans 12:2 ~

Lord, I did it again. I took another wrong turn, fell down one more time. I wonder if I'll ever get on the right track in the way I should go. Sometimes I'm not even aware that I'm about to fall into a trap until I've done it and feel the shame of my disgraceful behavior.

Father, I ask Your forgiveness for being such a disappointment to You. I pray that You would transform the way I think and make me a new person. I pray that You would show me the way to honor You in all I do. I am miserable each time I do something that displeases You. I'm sorry to be so weak.

Strengthen and renew me in Your love and grace.
Amen.

Failure is the opportunity to begin again more intelligently.

~ Henry Ford ~

July 21

Standing on the Promises!

All of God's promises have been fulfilled in Him. That is why we say "Amen" when we give glory to God through Christ.

~ 2 Corinthians 1:20 ~

Father, thank You for being faithful to Your promises. I believe that You will accomplish all that You intend in this world and that even through me some of Your work will be done.

I thank You for being such a loving part of my life and for allowing me to embrace You in every aspect of my being. You are my light in the darkest hours and my comfort when my soul aches. You are my Savior and I stand confidently on Your promises, for my life depends on You. *Amen.*

The main hinge on which faith turns is this: we must not imagine that the Lord's promises are true objectively but not in our experience. We must make them ours by embracing them in our hearts.

~ John Calvin ~

My Plans and Yours

When people do not accept divine guidance, they run wild. But whoever obeys the law is happy.
~ Proverbs 29:18 ~

Lord, I know that my plans don't always match Your plans. I pray today that I would seek Your divine guidance in all I do and in all I hope to do in the future.

I know that I sometimes set lofty goals and then forget to prepare an adequate foundation for them to prosper. Help me to ground the thoughts and plans I make according to Your will and purpose.

I pray for all Your children who seek Your help in the efforts they make, and who trust in You as they build foundations for their lives. We know that only You can truly guide our way no matter how many steps we take. Nothing can be built on our own, for we always need You as the foundation stone. Thank You for being part of our plans. *Amen.*

But the plans of the LORD stand firm forever,
the purposes of His heart through all generations.
~ Psalm 33:11 NIV ~

Because You Know Me

Live in such a way that God's love can bless you as you wait for the eternal life that our Lord Jesus Christ in His mercy is going to give you.

~ Jude 21 ~

Lord, I can hardly understand what it actually means that You know me. You know everything about me and yet You love me. You know my purpose, my worthiness, and the many times I fail You.

I pray that I might live in a way that offers a glimpse of You to others. I pray that my little light might shine brighter as we come to know each other more.

Lord, I pray to walk more closely with You and to talk with You more often. You know all that You want me to be and I pray for Your grace and guidance in all I do. *Amen.*

Search me, O God, and know my heart;
test me and know my anxious thoughts.
See if there is any offensive way in me,
and lead me in the way everlasting.

~ Psalm 139:23-24 NIV ~

July 24

Get Ready! Get Set! Go!

Get ready; be prepared!
~ Ezekiel 38:7 ~

Lord, I know that You have given us instructions to prepare the way for You. Just as You once sent John the Baptist into the wilderness to prepare the way for Jesus, You send us out too.

Your people are everywhere on this planet, creating new paths, sharing their hearts, offering Your hope. I ask that You would be with each person who prepares the way for Jesus to return to earth. I ask that You would open the eyes and ears of those who are yet on the fringe of understanding, and help them to grasp the meaning of Your return.

I pray for a surge of Your Holy Spirit to electrify all who speak in Your name or who write for Your glory. Help all of us, Lord, to be prepared for You each moment of every day. *Amen.*

It's better to prepare and prevent,
than to repair and repent.
~ Anonymous ~

Gold Stars!

"But you are to be perfect, even as your Father in heaven is perfect."

~ Matthew 5:48 ~

Lord, I remember back in grade school how nice it was to get a gold star for accomplishing a goal or doing the right thing. It was always fun to see how many stars I could earn.

I guess I haven't forgotten that mind set when it comes to my work for You. I'd love to think I could do something well enough to achieve a gold star from You. I'd like to even create a pattern of stars that could be accomplished over the rest of my life.

I know that gold stars or all the stars in heaven really have little to do with the light only You can give my soul, so I thank You for that light most of all. Bless all who seek Your light always. *Amen.*

Twelve stars for reaching the highest perfection: love of God, love of neighbor, obedience, chastity, poverty, attendance at choir, penance, humility, mortification, prayer, silence, peace.

~ St. John of the Cross ~

July 26

I Hope! I Hope! I Hope!

If we look forward to something we don't have yet, we must wait patiently and confidently.
~ Romans 8:25 ~

Lord, You know I'm always hoping for something … a new possibility, a new friendship, a resolution of an old problem. I raise up all I have to You in hope because my confidence about anything in this life rests with You. You are the hope of the world!

Today, I pray for everyone who places their hope and their confidence in You and who wait patiently for the answers to their prayers. I pray that You would draw near to each one who humbly puts their requests before You in the hope that You would illuminate their cause.

Father, we have only one hope for each of us as individuals, and for our planet. It all rests on You! That is the thing that always gives me hope. *Amen.*

Hope is not the conviction that something
will turn out well, but the certainty that something
makes sense, regardless of how it turns out.
~ Václav Havel ~

Restored, Revived, Renewed!

*What this means is that those who become Christians
become new persons. They are not the same anymore,
for the old life is gone. A new life has begun!*
~ 2 Corinthians 5:17 ~

Lord, I need a revival, a new beginning in my heart
and soul. I need to reconnect with You in new ways
that would refresh my energy and create new opportunities to grow and prosper in Your care.

For some reason, I haven't felt fully connected to
You as I once was. I haven't had the desire to give
You all I am or all I do. I pray for Your forgiveness
for my apathy and ask that You would restore me
to Yourself because of Your Son, Jesus. I believe that
You have more for me, and that with a renewed heart
and mind I might accomplish new dreams for You.
Restore me to Your grace and mercy. *Amen.*

*A revival is nothing else than a new
beginning of obedience to God.*
~ Charles G. Finney ~

Am I a Minister?

And I said, "Lord, I'll go! Send me."
~ Isaiah 6:8 ~

Lord God, I pray for all people who serve in some capacity as ministers around the globe. I pray that the fresh wind of Your Spirit would blow in their midst and revive their missions. I pray that You would keep building Your church around the world to create a Holy Fire of Your forgiveness, Your grace, and Your sovereignty.

Help each of us to be ministers to each other wherever we might be. Grant us wisdom and mercy. Help us raise each other up and set the light of Your love in every window. Be our guide and our mighty wind.

I pray that when You call, I would have the strength to answer. I pray that I would believe as so many others who are with me today and who came before me, to have the nerve and the desire to say to You, "I'm here, Lord. Send me!" *Amen.*

Blessed is he who comes in the name of the LORD.
~ Psalm 118:26 NIV ~

July 29

Your Light Is
On … In Me!

Clothe yourselves with the armor of right living, as those who live in the light.
~ Romans 13:12 ~

Lord, I love Your light. Any of Your light that shines through my soul illuminates me like nothing else can. I pray that You would help me turn up the light so that I am simply set aglow by Your love.

Help me then to shine that light for all the world to see. Help me to never be ashamed of the gospel of Christ, or the small part I might have in helping others to learn more about You. I am Your servant and Your child. It is such an honor to be part of You and an awesome thing to know that You are part of me. Lord, I pray for all who work to bring Your name to light, to light up the world with Your love and to recharge the hearts and minds of a dark humanity. I ask this in Jesus' name. *Amen.*

He who lives up to a little light shall have more light.
~ Thomas Brooks ~

July 30

Risky Business

Why should we ourselves be continually risking our lives, facing death hour by hour?
~ 1 Corinthians 15:30 ~

Father, most of us are not in peril for our very lives as many of the early Christians were. Yes, there are places in the world where believers risk their lives to tell others about You. Those people are our heroes.

I pray though for those of us who aren't at risk for life and limb, and yet we still play it safe. We guard our activities around our friends so that we don't come on too strong, or seem too caught up in all that we believe.

Help us to dare to be different. Help us to cast a wide net of vision, of purpose and of truth so that we begin a swarm, a new revival of Your love among the people. *Amen.*

Be daring, be different, be impractical; be anything
that will assert integrity of purpose and imaginative
vision against the play-it-safers, the creatures of the
commonplace, the slaves of the ordinary.
~ Cecil Beaton ~

Watch Thou, dear Lord,
with those who wake,
or watch, or weep tonight,
and give Thine angels
charge over those who sleep.
Tend Thy sick ones, Lord Christ.
Rest Thy weary ones.
Bless Thy dying ones.
Soothe Thy suffering ones.
Pity Thine afflicted ones.
Shield Thy joyous ones.
And all, for Thy love's sake.
Amen.

St. Augustine

August

Respect and Love

Show respect for everyone. Love your Christian brothers and sisters. Fear God. Show respect for the king.

~ 1 Peter 2:17 ~

Father, respect seems to have lost its meaning in our current culture. We used to have more honor for each other, respecting our elders, and respecting the rights of people to live as they would feel led to live. Today, it seems that few people even understand a word like respect and fewer still give it the place of honor it once had.

I pray for all of us to be more aware of each other's choices, to honor those choices and to respect any differences in thought or action or lifestyle that might exist. We are all Your children and You are the only God of this universe. Help us to be drawn to each other in respect and in love. *Amen.*

Without respect, love cannot go far or rise high;
it is an angel with but one wing.
~ Alexandre Dumas ~

August 1

Rescue Me!

Help me, O Lord my God; save me in accordance with Your love.

~ Psalm 109:26 NIV ~

Lord, I draw close to You when I'm in pain or when I'm in sorrow. I get swept away in lonely hours and wonder why life has taken the turn it has. Yet, each time, I'm aware of Your presence in a way that I don't always recognize when things are going well.

I know You have said to give thanks in all circumstances, and so I do thank You. I thank You that no matter what I'm going through, no matter how I feel, that You're there. Your presence is not based on how I feel, but on what You know I need and You know I need You all the time.

Please be with all who are lonely, or ill, or simply feel defeated by life. *Amen.*

The Lord protects the simplehearted;
when I was in great need, He saved me.
~ Psalm 116:6 NIV ~

August 2

The Blame Game

It was the woman You gave me who brought me the fruit, and I ate it." Then the LORD God asked the woman, "How could you do such a thing?" "The serpent tricked me," she replied.
~ Genesis 3:12-13 ~

Lord, one of the hardest things about life is the desire to not take responsibility for our own actions.

Sometimes I fall into the trap of thinking "if only" kinds of things. I imagine "if only" I had different parents, or "if only" I had married the other person. I know that the outcomes of my life have more to do with my choices and my distance from You when I make those choices, than they have to do with other people.

Help us, Lord, to stand firm with You any time we find ourselves in the garden and take the blame for the things we do. Forgive us then and help us move on. I ask this in Jesus' name. *Amen.*

It is better to take refuge in the
LORD than to trust in man.
~ Psalm 118:8 NIV ~

August 3

Bless the Children

The father of godly children has cause for joy. What a pleasure it is to have wise children. So give your parents joy! May she who gave you birth be happy.
~ Proverbs 23:24-25 ~

Lord, some babies come into this world with a lot of fanfare, a lot of expectation, and a lot of love. Some babies come into this world and are nearly invisible from the day they are born.

I pray that You would wrap Your arms around all the precious children in this world and give them at least one human heart to love them, one special person to guide their steps and protect them, and one place where they feel safe and strong. Guide each parent to love their child in the best ways to build on the potential You designed within them. Help us all to welcome children with hearts of joy.

Amen.

Sons are a heritage from the LORD,
children a reward from Him.
~ Psalm 127:3 NIV ~

What Does God Want from Me?

What does the LORD your God require of you? He requires you to fear Him, to live according to His will, to love and worship Him with all your heart and soul, and to obey the LORD's commands and laws.

~ Deuteronomy 10:12-13 ~

Lord, You've been pretty clear about what You want from Your children. I am certain that Your ways are the blessed ways, that bring me greater possibility and strength and keep me on a straight path.

Father, I ask now that You would help me to be wise, to seek You in all things and to obey You because I love You. Help me to be a worthy child, someone You can trust with Your incredible truth. I ask this in the name of my Lord, Jesus Christ. *Amen.*

The tiniest fragment of obedience, and heaven opens up and the profoundest truths of God are yours straight away. God will never reveal more truth about Himself till you obey what you know already.

~ Oswald Chambers ~

August 5

Why We Pray

Confess your sins to each other and pray for each other so that you may be healed. The earnest prayer of a righteous person has great power and wonderful results.

~ James 5:16 ~

Lord, I like to think of myself as a prayer person, someone who comes to You for all the details of my life. Yet, I know that I do not pray nearly enough.

Forgive me for being such a weak instrument of prayer. I ask today that You would put Your fire into the hearts of all who seek You and impress them with the possibilities that prayer brings.

Lord, grant that we might be close enough to Your sweet Spirit, to help things go right for ourselves and the people we love. *Amen.*

The LORD is near to all who call on Him, to all who call on Him in truth. He fulfills the desires of those who fear Him; He hears their cry and saves them.

~ Psalm 145:18-19 NIV ~

Thing One and Thing Two

Let heaven fill your thoughts. Do not think only about things down here on earth.
~ Colossians 3:2 ~

Lord, I know that I often get bogged down with the immediate needs of my household and my work, rather than setting priorities. Help me to choose You first in my thoughts and actions. Help me to set the priority to pray before I do anything else.

Fill my thoughts with those things that You desire for me. Help me to see clearly the steps to take and to do so with trust and joy. I ask You to help all who seek to put You first and have a desire to please You.

I pray for greater strength and wisdom in the ways I use my precious time here on earth. Thank You, Lord, for all Your guidance. *Amen.*

You can't get second things by putting them first; you can get second things only by putting first things first.
~ C. S. Lewis ~

August 7

Refresh My Spirit

But grow in the special favor and knowledge of our Lord and Savior Jesus Christ.
~ 2 Peter 3:18 ~

Father, I thank You for pushing me along sometimes. I thank You that I'm not truly comfortable or content to simply stay as I am. I know that contentment sometimes brings a kind of apathy for life. I pray to always desire more of You and more from myself.

I thank You for the favor You have shown me. I know that when I'm struggling, when things look bleak, that I can trust You to be with me, to help me find solutions, and to help me press on.

I want to be worthy of Your faithful love, Your undeserved mercy, and Your willingness to pick me up each time I fall. You are my light and my salvation and my spirit can only grow when I'm close to You. Renew me, Lord, according to Your will. *Amen.*

Create in me a pure heart, O God, and
renew a steadfast spirit within me.
~ Psalm 51:10 NIV ~

Love Each Other!

We love each other as a result of His loving us first.
~ 1 John 4:19 ~

Father, I forget what it means to truly love others as You have loved me. How do I want You to love me? Unconditionally! I want You to love me in spite of me, in spite of my shortcomings and my failures. I want You to love me as I am, but not be willing to let me remain in a place that is not good for me.

Help me, Lord, to be willing to love others in that same way. Help me to forgive those who offend me and to be gracious to those who do not realize how unkind they are.

As I walk with my family and my friends and neighbors on this day, help me to love them, truly love them, as You do. Help me to see You in their faces and in their actions. *Amen.*

The greatest happiness of life is the conviction
that we are loved – loved for ourselves, or
rather, loved in spite of ourselves.
~ Victor Hugo ~

August 9

A Touch of Honey

*This is what the L*ORD *Almighty says: "Judge fairly and honestly, and show mercy and kindness to one another."*

~ *Zechariah 7:9* ~

Lord, I believe You've given all of us the ability to be kind. You've graced us with enough honey to share with those we love and those we don't yet call our friends.

We've forgotten to be kind to one another. We forget who we are in You. We forget that each person is fighting a personal battle and that some days are harder than others.

The one thing that might make a difference is a small act of kindness, some simple willingness to be giving. I pray that You would remind me wherever I am today, to serve up a scoop of kindness at every opportunity. Bless those who bless others even with a smile today. *Amen.*

*Because Your love is better than
life, my lips will glorify You.*
~ *Psalm 63:3* NIV ~

August 10

Praying for Enemies

*"God blesses you when you are mocked and persecuted
and lied about because you are My followers. Be happy
about it! Be very glad! For a great reward awaits you
in heaven."*

~ Matthew 5:11-12 ~

Father, forgive me if I have offended anyone and caused them to become my enemy. Forgive my uncaring heart and bless the person I offended in every possible way. For those people who are unknown enemies, I ask Your blessing as well. Pour out Your Spirit on their hearts so that they might see You and be turned to friends.

For those who go around this world, prowling and devouring the innocent, being merciless to the less fortunate, being knowingly wicked, I ask even more mercy. Only You have the power to change any of us, Lord. I pray for this change in all who are blind to You today. *Amen.*

*The will of God, to which the law gives expression, is
that men should defeat their enemies by loving them.*

~ Dietrich Bonhoeffer ~

Mountain Moving

Then Jesus told them, "I assure you, if you have faith and don't doubt, you can do things like this and much more. You can even say to this mountain, 'May God lift you up and throw you into the sea,' and it will happen. If you believe, you will receive whatever you ask for in prayer."

~ Matthew 21:21-22 ~

Father of all truth, we want so much to believe we can move mountains and that with You all things are possible, but we immediately reflect our fears into the things for which we pray.

When I pray for something that is truly important to me, I find that I hope, more than I believe without doubt. I hope You would be in agreement with my prayer. I hope I'm praying for something that is in accordance with Your will and purpose. I hope to somehow move a mountain. Help me to create "believing" prayers, ones that have no doubt mixed in. *Amen.*

You hear, O LORD, the desire of the afflicted;
You encourage them, and You listen to their cry.
~ Psalm 10:17 NIV ~

August 12

Finding a Happy Place

*Those who have reason to be thankful should
continually sing praises to the Lord.*
~ *James 5:13* ~

Lord, help me to learn to be happy in Your presence.
Help me to understand that You are always near me,
always able to see my situation and are fully ready
to help me any time at all. Help me to find true
happiness by spending more time with You, and by
seeing Your hand at work everywhere I go.

I pray to be more loving to those I meet, ready to
give from the heart and willing to help as I'm able
to. Bless all those who seek a spiritual happiness, a
contentment that comes only from walking closer to
You. I pray Your gifts of grace and mercy on each
aching heart, each weary soul, and each broken person that needs Your help today. Thank You for Your
faithfulness. *Amen.*

Keep me safe, O God, for in You I take refuge.
~ *Psalm 16:1 NIV* ~

I Surrender ... Again!

Don't copy the behaviors and customs of this world, but let God transform you into a new person by changing the way you think.
~ Romans 12:2 ~

Lord, so often I try to surrender myself to You, to give up things that tie me to the world and block my way to You. I know that to completely surrender would mean I've learned to trust You in all things and learned to be content.

I know I haven't arrived there, but I aspire to be more Yours than I am today. Pardon those stubborn parts of me that resist giving in. I am Your child and there is nowhere else I'd rather be than in Your care and keeping.

Help me to lift the white flag of surrender, so that I might complete my work on earth in Your grace. Bless all who wish to surrender their hearts to You today. *Amen.*

I will sing to the Lord for He has been good to me.
~ Psalm 13:6 NIV ~

Undefeated!

*"Here on earth you will have many trials and sorrow.
But take heart, because I have overcome the world."*
~ *John 16:33* ~

Lord, there are days when I feel like a champion, like nothing can stop me because I am strong and I know exactly where I'm going. I thank You for those days because I know they come wholly from You. Unfortunately, those are not as often my experience as I wish they were.

Lord, forgive my faulty thinking. I trust You. I believe in You and You alone are my hope and the One who creates the opportunity for victory.

Help me, Father, to keep my eyes on You so that I can know You are leading the way to all possibility. Thank You for giving me endless reasons to keep my hopes high. *Amen.*

*Never talk defeat. Use words like hope,
belief, faith, victory.*
~ *Norman Vincent Peale* ~

Turning up the Heat!

Jacob panted, "I will not let You go unless you bless me." "What is your name?" the man asked. He replied, "Jacob." "Your name will no longer be Jacob," the man told him. "It is now Israel," because you have struggled with both God and men and have won."
~ Genesis 32:26-28 ~

Lord, I guess most of us have struggled, wrestling with You in some way or another. Unlike Jacob, we have not always held on for the blessing.

Lord, help us to stand up for those things we truly believe and to wait with all joy for Your blessing. Help us to trust that You have already given us new names and new hearts on that day when we chose to be born anew in Your Spirit.

Be with all who wrestle with life and cannot stand up against it. Let us not grow weary of making the effort to keep trying and become what we are capable of becoming. *Amen.*

To become what we are capable
of becoming is the only end in life.
~ Robert Louis Stevenson ~

Keep On Trying

Be strong and steady, always enthusiastic about the Lord's work, for you know that nothing you do for the Lord is ever useless.

~ 1 Corinthians 15:58 ~

Lord, thank You for picking me up when I fall down and helping me get started all over again. I know I couldn't do anything without Your strength and guidance.

Sometimes I try too hard and other times I know I don't try enough, but I do yearn to be better and to do better. I know that my efforts will not make You love me more, for You have chosen to love me in spite of me.

Be with all Your children who try to come closer to You and to do Your will. I pray that You would bless their work and their intentions and keep them safely in Your care. Help us, Father, to desire to try, and try again. *Amen.*

He who goes out weeping, carrying seed to sow, will return with songs of joy, carrying sheaves with him.

~ Psalm 126:6 NIV ~

When I Go Astray

All of us have strayed away like sheep. We have left God's paths to follow our own.
~ Isaiah 53:6 ~

Father, forgive me when I wander away from You. I pray that You would not allow me to get too far from Your side and that You would always bring me back and hold on to me. I ask You to help me dismiss the noises of the world, the distractions and temptations that assail me and fill my heart instead with Your Spirit.

I pray for all the prodigal sons and daughters who have walked away from You and who seek even now to find the path home again. Be with each one of them and return them to Your favor. In Jesus' name, I pray. *Amen.*

I have strayed like a lost sheep. Seek Your servant,
for I have not forgotten Your commands.
~ Psalm 119:176 NIV ~

Human Beings,
or Human Doings

Don't you realize that all of you together are the temple of God and that the Spirit of God lives in you?
~ 1 Corinthians 3:16 ~

Lord, I know that I can't sit still. I'm always up and running to do mundane things that need to get done, but I'm not always sure if those things are important to You. Help me to slow down and just be a human being …

It's hard for me to imagine what it must be like to see Your children scurrying about, doing, doing, doing and hardly realizing You're there. How can You exist in a temple that doesn't invite You in to be at its center? Father, forgive us when our doing gets in the way of our being. Help us seek to fill our days well and to remember to make more room for You in all we do. *Amen.*

It is not that doing is unimportant. It is rather that right doing springs from right being.
~ Robert Llewelyn ~

August 19

Wait for Me!

"Jesus has been taken away from you into heaven. And someday, just as you saw Him go, He will return!"
~ Acts 1:11 ~

Father, we wait in hope for those things that would ease life's pains. We wait for prayers to be answered and for doors to open. Sometimes we pray for the same person, or the same situation, or the same dream over and over again. We wait season after season for the prayer to be answered.

You know that when we wait so long, in our humanness, we get discouraged and we wonder if the prayer will ever be answered.

I ask that You would be with all who wait for You. Some even now have waited years for You to heed their cry, some wait for You to return to claim Your bride, and some wait with simple childlike hope. Bless each of the ones who wait with love. *Amen.*

I wait for the LORD, my soul waits,
and in His word I put my hope.
~ Psalm 130:5 NIV ~

Food for Thought

Fix your thoughts on what is true and honorable and right. Think about things that are pure and lovely and admirable. Think about things that are excellent and worthy of praise.

~ Philippians 4:8 ~

Lord, I'm not quite sure why, but when it comes to the things that we could truly feast our thoughts upon, we go for the scraps and the moldy ideas, instead of the more beautiful, more sacred, more humble offerings that You have for us. Deliver our thoughts from evil, Lord, and help us to focus our attention on those things that will give us a better grasp of who we are, and who You are.

Help us to desire the banquet of delights that only You can give so that our parched souls may not thirst and our spirits may be satisfied. I pray for all those who believe in You and ask You to guide their thoughts toward heaven today. *Amen.*

A Christian is a person who thinks in believing and believes in thinking.

~ St. Augustine ~

August 21

Harvest Time

Worship and serve Him with your whole heart and with a willing mind. For the Lord sees every heart and understands and knows every plan and thought. If you seek Him, you will find Him.
~ 1 Chronicles 28:9 ~

Lord, help me to sow the good seeds of Your love in my own heart and into the lives of those around me. Help me to be willing to work through the dry spells, the storms, and the weeds of discontent.

Let me be aware of Your kindness and mercy, to give each seed the growing room to become all that it is meant to be. Help me to gather the flowers of grace in joy and to share them even with those around me.

Lord, bless us with a harvest of truth, a spirit that is ready to grow. Bless each person who strives to grow strong and faithful and let each one harvest Your gifts in great joy. *Amen.*

We must not hope to be mowers, And to gather the ripe old ears, Let us, therefore, not be weary of well-doing; for we shall reap an eternal harvest of comfort, if we faint not.
~ George Whitefield ~

On with the Search

"If you look for Me in earnest, you will find Me when you seek Me. I will be found by you," says the LORD.
~ *Jeremiah 29:13-14* ~

Lord, I seek You with all my heart. I pray, Father, that I would seek the truth of You, not the one I hope for, but the glorious, gracious, unexplainable and yet knowable God of my heart. I know I have only had a glimpse of You and I long to see You more clearly.

I pray for the ones who seek You today. I pray for those with concerns for loved ones or who have simply lost their way in a confusing world. I ask that You would draw near to each one.

Thank You for loving us beyond any sense of definition we may have, for laying down Your life for us, and for being steadfast and true. *Amen.*

There's a God we want and there's a God who is and they are not the same God. The turning point comes when we stop seeking the God we want and start seeking the God who is.
~ *Patrick M. Morley* ~

August 23

Who Am I?

Examine yourselves to see if your faith is really genuine. Test yourselves. If you cannot tell that Jesus Christ is among you, it means you have failed the test.
~ 2 Corinthians 13:5 ~

Lord, I seek to understand more of who I am in relationship to You. I look inward and hope to discover more of the mystery that connects me to You, that sweet sense of knowing that gives me a taste of Your truth.

I ask that You would continue to share Your light with me and shape me even in my darkness. I am Your instrument, Your child.

Lord, help me to know more of who I am so that I can turn up the light for others in a way that helps them also test their faith. We crave to have more of the luster of You in all we do. *Amen.*

Frequent combing gives the hair more luster and makes it easier to comb; a soul that frequently examines its thoughts, words, and deeds, which are its hair, doing all things for the love of God, will have lustrous hair.
~ St. John of the Cross ~

August 24

Life Celebration

*Give thanks to the L*ORD *and proclaim His greatness.*
Let the whole world know what He has done.
~ 1 Chronicles 16:8 ~

Lord, in all my hurry to understand this life, I sometimes forget to celebrate the fact that I live at all. The more I know of You, the more I celebrate the joys You bring to Your children and proclaim Your greatness to others.

You are the Source of all that is and I celebrate knowing You have taken such a personal interest in all of Your creation. I pray that the good will always outweigh the bad and that good will triumph with Your guidance and according to Your will and purpose.

I celebrate my life. I celebrate the lives of those around me who help me to become more than I would ever be without them, and I celebrate Your grace. Thank You for this precious gift of life. *Amen.*

Life is not a holiday, but an education. And the one
eternal lesson for us all is how better we can love.
~ Henry Drummond ~

August 25

God Restores Me

Even the wilderness will rejoice in those days. The desert will blossom with flowers. Yes, there will be an abundance of flowers and singing and joy!
~ Isaiah 35:1-2 ~

Lord, when I look back on those times in my life when I only produced weeds, when I failed to heed Your call or live up to Your dreams for me, I cringe.

But joy comes when I realize that You found a way to bring me back, to embrace me and to give me the opportunity to thrive and grow again. You planted me safely in Your garden and nothing can change that. I may produce more weeds, but I'm on holy ground and I'm living in Your mercy and grace.

Please forgive those things that distance me from You and that keep me from blossoming. Forgive those things that drain all the color from my life and make everything seem gray. Thank You for restoring me to Yourself with great love. *Amen.*

*Rise up and help us; redeem us
because of Your unfailing love.*
~ Psalm 44:26 NIV ~

August 26

Rust Removal

Give all your worries and cares to God, for He cares about what happens to you.
~ 1 Peter 5:7 ~

Lord, here I am again in need of a little extra polish because I'm rusting away under my own weight of worry. I think it all depends on me. Well, I know that it depends on me, when I depend on You.

I ask today that You would scrape away my worn out, rusty thinking and polish my faith so that I leave all things in Your hand. You know what is best for me and You know the big picture, the best route that gets me where You need me to go.

Remove the rust of worry and help me to rest in Your grace and be peaceful there. Fill me with praise for all that is yet to be. Thank You, Lord, for renewing my life and my spirit. *Amen.*

Anxiety is the rust of life, destroying its brightness and weakening its power. A childlike and abiding trust in Providence is its best preventive and remedy.
~ Anonymous ~

August 27

Humility and Honor

So humble yourselves under the mighty power of God,
and in His good time He will honor you.
~ 1 Peter 5:6 ~

Lord, I won't deny that I sometimes hope to do something noteworthy, something that my peers will delight in and even reward. I guess we all like to feel we've done a job well and that someone notices our efforts.

Father, give us grace to shine in Your light, to humbly receive and humbly give of the gifts and talents You have bestowed upon us.

Be with all those who mistakenly think that climbing the ladder of success will give them everything they desire. Help us to understand that all honor and praise can only be given through alignment with Your call on our lives. I honor and praise You with all my heart. *Amen.*

Just as anyone who climbs a rotten ladder risks his life,
so are honors and power a danger for humility.
~ St. John Climacus ~

August 28

Lost and Found

"Heaven will be happier over one lost sinner who returns to God than over ninety-nine who are righteous and haven't strayed away!"
~ Luke 15:7 ~

Lord, I know that on any given day, I hinge on being a lost soul. Yes, I realize that You have already claimed me and because of Your great mercy, You will not let me stray too far from You. Perhaps, I simply feel lost some days.

I pray today for all who either are lost or who feel lost that You would reach out to them, running toward them with Your smile of grace and Your holy love.

Forgive us when we step away from You, when we get lost in the streets of humanity and forget that we are heavenly children. Forgive us when we forget who we are. Thank You for finding me so long ago and for holding tightly to my spirit. *Amen.*

There is no one so far lost that Jesus cannot find him and cannot save him.
~ Andrew Murray ~

August 29

Planning a Course

I know, LORD, that a person's life is not his own. No one is able to plan his own course.
~ Jeremiah 10:23 ~

Lord, You know I'm always making lists and plans and setting new goals. It seems to be part of my nature to like to imagine some new dream and go after it. After all, You set this world in motion and made it everybody's goal to discover You are there and to reclaim a life with You through Jesus.

Sometimes, I forget this life is not my own. In fact, from anything I can tell, none of it is truly in my control. You are the Author and the Inventor of all I will ever be.

I thank You for being with me at every age and stage. I thank You that You have an exquisite plan for me and if I stay on the path, together we'll make it happen. Thank You for planning such an incredible journey for me. *Amen.*

Aim at heaven and you will get earth thrown in:
aim at earth and you will get neither.
~ C. S. Lewis ~

August 30

Instruct Me!

People who despise advice will find themselves in trouble; those who respect it will succeed.
~ *Proverbs 13:13* ~

Lord, I thank You for being the most significant teacher in my life. You have provided real-life examples to show me the way. You bring to mind those snares and obstacles that have caused others to fall so that I can avoid similar traps.

Help me to be open to Your advice in all that I do so that I may prosper according to Your plans for my good. I ask today that You would be with all those who seek Your guidance and give them concrete understanding of what You desire for them. I pray for those who seek You to be open to Your wisdom and to heed Your counsel. Help all of us, Lord, to always receive Your instruction with joy. *Amen.*

"I will instruct you and teach you in the way you should go; I will counsel you and watch over you."
~ *Psalm 32:8 NIV* ~

August 31

My dearest Lord,
Be Thou a bright flame before me,
Be Thou a guiding star above me,
Be Thou a smooth path beneath me,
Be Thou a kindly shepherd behind me,
Today – tonight – and forever!

~ Columba ~

September

P. R. A. Y. – Persevere. Reflect. Act. Yield.

Patient endurance is what you need now, so you will continue to do God's will. Then you will receive all that He has promised.
~ Hebrews 10:36 ~

Lord, sometimes when I pray, I want to climb onto Your lap and tell You everything about me, everything that hurts or makes me glad.

Other times I'm afraid to come close to You, for fear that I've offended You in some way or that I've grieved Your heart by my actions. My prayers seem distant when I feel like that.

I love knowing that You are there no matter how I feel. You receive me when I'm the better me, and when I'm the worst possible me. Thank You for being near me when I pray. *Amen.*

Tell God what is in your heart,
as one unloads one's heart, its
pleasures and its pains, to a dear friend.
~ François Fénelon ~

It's All Providence

To all who believed Him and accepted Him, He gave the right to become children of God.
~ John 1:12 ~

Lord, thank You for what You have so willingly provided for me from Your hand. Thank You for a home that is safe and warm. Thank You for the people who surround me with love and offer me encouragement and support.

From Your hand, Lord, all things are made manifest. I ask that You would continue to draw near to me and to those I love, providing what we need to help sustain life. I pray for those who do not have enough, for those who are homeless and severely impoverished, and ask that You would open the hearts of many to provide for them. *Amen.*

He set the earth on its foundations;
it can never be moved.
~ Psalm 104:5 NIV ~

September 2

Spirit Power

Now all glory to God, who is able, through His mighty power at work within us, to accomplish infinitely more than we might ask or think.
~ Ephesians 3:20 ~

Lord, I have to confess that I am drawn to the joyful idea of unleashing whatever power You would have my soul possess so that I could work for the good of people in this world. I long for those opportunities.

At the same time, I fear them. I fear that I am either not worthy or too timid to take on the kind of power that would fuel the spirits of others. I'm afraid that if I try to do that, I'll let You down or even cause someone to move farther away from You.

Lord, You know what You want to accomplish through me. Help me to simply be open to Your calling and willing to step out in faith according to Your will and purpose. *Amen.*

The highest conceivable state of spirituality is produced by a concentration of all the powers and passions of the soul upon the person of Christ.
~ Charles H. Spurgeon ~

September 3

Just a Kind Word

Kind words are like honey — sweet to the soul and healthy for the body.
~ Proverbs 16:24 ~

Lord, when I imagine what impact words might have, I only have to stop and realize that You actually spoke the world into existence. At Your word, the physical aspects of this planet came into being.

I know how devastating unkind words can be, causing greater damage sometimes than physical abuse. We should be more careful about what we say. I wonder why we don't understand that we help to create those things that are spoken.

I pray that kind words might be heard by those who feel invisible. I pray that kind words would heal the heart of every person whose spirit feels broken, and I pray that kind words would encourage them and the people I love. Help me to be much kinder today to everyone around me. *Amen.*

Kind words can be short and easy to speak,
but their echoes are truly endless.
~ Mother Teresa ~

September 4

On a Wing and a Prayer

So I pray that God, who gives you hope, will keep you happy and full of peace as you believe in Him.
~ Romans 15:13 ~

Lord, nothing can really replace the hope that fills our hearts. We turn to You in every life circumstance, praying for Your favor, Your healing, and Your comfort. We know that on our own, we live on a wing and a prayer, flying from hope to hope.

Be with all those who put their hope in You. I pray that today they would stand on that hope, rely on it, and trust You as the author of all that is good. It is not easy in a world that is crumbling, or when our own circumstances are falling apart, to trust that there is more.

You are the hope of the world and we look forward to all that You bring to our lives. Comfort us and renew us with Your precious Spirit on wings of love. *Amen.*

The natural flights of the human mind are not from pleasure to pleasure, but from hope to hope.
~ Samuel Johnson ~

What Is Success?

Commit your actions to the LORD, and your plans will succeed.

~ Proverbs 16:3 ~

Lord, forgive me for any of those moments when I falsely believe that my success is of my own doing. Forgive me when I forget to commit my work to You. I know that I have no power on this earth, no talent, no successful enterprise that does not come from Your hand. I can do nothing without You and so I thank You for Your tremendous grace and mercy.

We prize independence, sometimes so much that we forget to surrender all that we have and all that we are to You. It is only in the process of true surrender that we can come to know genuine success. Help us to always want only the success You want for us. Bless all who commit their work and their lives to You. *Amen.*

We have forgotten the gracious hand which has preserved us in peace, and multiplied and enriched and strengthened us.
~ Abraham Lincoln ~

September 6

Me? Stubborn?

"The hearts of these people are hardened, and their ears cannot hear."

~ Acts 28:27 ~

Lord, forgive me when I'm so stubborn that I can't hear Your voice or see what You have planned for me. I like to think that I am pliable and soft, ready any time to embrace Your Spirit and to follow You through the day. I like to think that, but it is not always true.

I see now that there are many times and even some areas of my life where I am stubbornly hoping to remain in control, not totally willing to surrender everything I am and everything I might be to You. Forgive my hardness of heart. Perhaps I too could have "stubborn" as a middle name.

Father, since You have called me by name to be Your own child, I stand in Your mercy and in Your grace, asking You to heal me of a calloused heart, so that I might live fully and lovingly for You. *Amen.*

Stubbornness should have been my middle name.
~ Martin Luther ~

Standing on the Rock

Do I have the strength of a stone? Is my body made of bronze? No, I am utterly helpless, without any chance of success.

~ Job 6:12-13 ~

Lord, I am so vulnerable. Let the winds change and my attention shift, let my finances fall, and I'm undone. Let friends betray me and I wonder what is left.

How amazing it is to realize that we are utterly helpless without You. You are the only Rock that can hold us up when we're shaky; the only refuge when we're weary.

I pray today to be so suited in Your armor that nothing can harm me; that nothing can change the course You have set. I pray for all those who seek to stand on the Rock of Your salvation and love. Help us to shine our armor and go forth in joy, knowing that we are totally surrounded by Your great love. *Amen.*

*It is not armor as armor, but as armor of God,
that makes the soul impregnable.*
~ William Gurnall ~

September 8

Hold on Tight!

Let us hold tightly without wavering to the hope we say we affirm, for God can be trusted to keep His promise.

~ Hebrews 10:23 ~

Lord, sometimes the only prayer I can think of is "Help!" when I find myself drowning in the sorrows I've created myself. I know I am the one who is most responsible for the things that have not yet gone as I intended. You have been faithful to me. You always give me a chance to try again, to rise from the depths of my own despair and seek Your face.

Today, I thank You for being with me and helping me to hold on tightly to Your promises. I know that You are there for me each time I reach out, each time I reach up for You. Bless all who hold on to You and stand on Your promises. *Amen.*

When I find that so much of my life has stolen unprofitably away, why do I yet try to resolve again? I try, because reformation is necessary and despair is criminal. I try, in humble hope of the help of God.

~ Samuel Johnson ~

September 9

That's Amazing!

There are three things that amaze me – no, four things I do not understand: how an eagle glides through the sky, how a snake slithers on a rock, how a ship navigates the ocean, how a man loves a woman.
~ Proverbs 30:18-19 ~

Lord, I guess the author of Proverbs would be awed by space rockets, cell phones, and the Internet. How a man loves a woman and real love in the heart of human beings is certainly still an amazing thing.

You have provided us with no end of opportunities to be awed by Your work. If we witness the power of a waterfall or the tenderness of baby kittens, or we hear the kindness in the words of a stranger, or see acts of charity, we can still be amazed.

Help us to be awed at what You have provided for us, the things that You have put in our hands. I ask for Your love, Your mercy and Your guidance … things that truly amaze me. *Amen.*

The way you see life will largely determine what you get out of it.
~ Zig Ziglar ~

September 10

Living in Love

God is love, and all who live in love live in God, and God lives in them. And as we live in God, our love grows more perfect.

~ 1 John 4:16-17 ~

Lord, we are such novices at understanding love. We walk around with our hearts on our sleeves, or we build walls against love because we fear it.

Father, thank You for love. Help us to seek love that causes us to grow and gives us a greater desire to become lovable.

We are not good at love. Our hearts long to have more of the love You offer us. You know what we need at every hour because You are so close to us and watch over us with Your generous and giving Spirit. Help us love each other with a similar spirit. Help us to seek to know everything we can about what love really is. We know that perfect love drives fear away, so please help us to love more fully. *Amen.*

Jesus Christ founded His empire upon love;
and at this hour millions of men would die for Him.

~ Napoleon Bonaparte ~

As It Happens

"When someone has been given much, much will be required in return."

~ Luke 12:48 ~

Lord, Your Spirit is impacting the world in amazing ways. You've given me so much, so I know I need to be actively involved in the way people's hearts and minds are shaped. I am not asking for popularity or celebrity status, I'm just asking that I would be worthy of the work You have given me to do. I love being able to do that in my own simple ways.

Other times, I'm a person who watches as things around me happen and wonder if I missed something important, something I could have helped create.

As much as possible, Lord, please be with me and others who want to share Your great love. *Amen.*

People can be divided into three groups: 1. Those who make things happen., 2. Those who watch things happen, and 3. Those who wonder what's happening!

~ Anonymous ~

The Right Questions

Until I get there, focus on reading the Scriptures to the church, encouraging the believers, and teaching them.
~ 1 Timothy 4:13 ~

Lord, even though I don't often feel like I have the right answers for some of the circumstances life presents to me and those I love, I do think I'm getting better at asking the right questions. Perhaps the best question is, "How do I love You more?" A lot of answers instantly come to mind. I could do more for others, showing my love for You. I could love myself more and learn to trust You in all things. I could talk with You more so our relationship can grow.

Even when I don't have the answers, I ask that You would keep me aware of the questions. Give me a yearning to know how I can please You. Thank You for keeping me close to You. *Amen.*

Having the answers is not essential to living.
What is essential is the sense of God's
presence during dark seasons of questioning.
~ Ravi Zacharias ~

September 13

Don't Look Back

Put your hope in the LORD, for with the LORD is unfailing love and with Him is full redemption. He Himself will redeem Israel from all their sins.
~ Psalm 130:7-8 NIV ~

Lord, some of us are still stuck in past regrets. Help us to stop looking back as though we could somehow reverse the hands of the clock and change things. We cannot change the past, but You have blessed us with today. We can stop wasting our energy over days long gone, and invest ourselves in the future You have planned for us.

Please be with anyone today who is stuck in the past, who has become unwilling to keep moving out of fear of past sins. Forgive those sins and open new doors and windows for Your children to walk through and to see the light of what is ahead. *Amen.*

Regret for time wasted can become a power for good in the time that remains, if we will only stop the waste and the idle, useless regretting.
~ Arthur Brisbane ~

September 14

More Than a Dead Fish

There is salvation in no one else! God has given no other name under heaven by which we must be saved.
~ Acts 4:12 ~

Lord, thank You for breathing life into me. Thank You for being willing to rescue me from the depths of despair and oceans of deceit.

It's amazing that You've made it so easy for us to find You. You didn't create the ten-things–to-do-before-You-can-be-saved list.

You made it simple. You asked us to love You and believe in You and trust You and You would do the same for us right back. We seldom can find even an earthly relationship where we can get that much joy. You are the breath of life and I am humbled by what You've done for me. With all my heart, I thank You for offering me the sweet and simple path to salvation. *Amen.*

From the Lord comes deliverance.
May Your blessing be on Your people.
~ Psalm 3:8 NIV ~

Risk and Reward

"God blesses you when people mock you and persecute
you and lie about you because you are My followers."
~ Matthew 5:11-12 ~

Lord, it is always difficult to step outside a safety net. Most of us want to feel comfortable about our plans and ideas before we execute them. Sometimes the only way to achieve Your purposes is for us to take a leap of faith and trust You for the result.

Today, I pray for all those who walk in faith and step up boldly to the task of sharing Your love with others. I pray that they will rejoice with You in all that brings glory to Your name. Bless the speakers, and the writers; bless the ministers and the missionaries. Help each person who takes a little risk for You to be daring and fulfilled in achieving their purpose. Help us to take the risk and share the reward of Your great love. *Amen.*

We will shout for joy when You are victorious and
will lift up our banners in the name of our God.
~ Psalm 20:5 NIV ~

September 16

Healing and Happiness

The Lord's healing power was strongly with Jesus.
~ Luke 5:17 ~

Lord, thank You for sustaining us with good health and strong bodies. We know that when we are struck with illness, everything else pales in comparison to our desire to be healthy again.

Remind us on those days when we are taking life for granted, pursuing happiness as though it was some kind of right we had earned, that our praise and honor all need to go to You. You are the One who cares for us in every way, granting us health and happiness.

I pray for all who suffer with any illness, whether chronic or temporary, that You would heal them and restore them to full strength because of Your steadfast love. I pray that those who are healthy would offer thanks and praise for all You do to keep them well. I seek Your blessings and favor, in Jesus' name. *Amen.*

All our difficulties are only platforms for the manifestation of His grace, power and love.
~ Hudson Taylor ~

September 17

Clouds and Fires

The LORD spread out a cloud as a covering, and a fire to give light at night.
~ *Psalm 105:39 NIV* ~

Father of all light, thank You for Your continual guidance. Help us when we approach the unknown places, the unfamiliar ground. Help us by providing a holy light to guide us on our way. Help us to see You in all that we do and to follow Your lead.

When we're parched and dry from moving along our own paths, grant us the mercy of Your covering of grace. Provide a rest from our blind direction and open up our hearts to desire to walk more closely with You. Be our pillar of cloud each day that we might find protection from those things that would scorch and wound us. Guide us into the dark of night with the true light of Your love. Help us always to seek Your guidance wherever and whenever we move to new ground. *Amen.*

Faith is the strength by which a shattered world shall emerge into the light.
~ *Helen Keller* ~

September 18

The Grudge Drudge

Let everything you say be good and helpful, so that your words will be an encouragement to those who hear them.

~ Ephesians 4:29 ~

Lord, forgive us when we carry a grudge against anyone, whether we have reason for it or not. Help us to see that allowing a root of bitterness to take hold of us only causes us to decay from the inside, damaging our spirits and preventing us from moving on in a positive direction. Bless those who offend us and help us to be willing to let go of the things that grieve us as quickly as we can.

Remind us to be more like You, willing to offer forgiveness that allows us to begin again. Inspire our hearts and minds to desire only good things for each other. Help us to forgive as we have been forgiven, remembering that we too have offended others. Free us of anything that creates a seed of bitterness in our hearts and minds. *Amen.*

The heaviest thing to carry is a grudge.

~ Anonymous ~

The To-Do List

*Make it your goal to live a quiet life, minding your
own business and working with your hands.*
~ 1 Thessalonians 4:11 ~

Lord, it feels like my "to-do" list gets longer every
day. Remind me that no matter how busy I am, the
best thing I can do is to start my day with You. I pray
for each activity on my list that I would accomplish it
for the good of my family and to Your glory.

I pray for others who strive to achieve goals today, whether those goals are big or small. I know that
sometimes even the simplest task can hang us up for
hours and make it nearly impossible to get anything
done. Remind us, Lord, that our main goal in life is
not to simply check things off our busy lists, but to
seek Your will for our lives in all we do. I pray that
You would guide all those I care about according to
Your grace and mercy. *Amen.*

*Lord, grant that I may always
desire more than I accomplish.*
~ Michelangelo ~

Patience and Virtue

Better to be patient than powerful; better to have self-control than to conquer a city.
~ Proverbs 16:32 ~

Lord, only You are the Potter who can help us become more useful vessels, remolding us to fit Your purpose in this world. Please be with us and speak to us in the stillness, that we might know Your direction and desire more of You. I pray for You to work in my life in ways that would help define me or create in me all that I can be for You. Help me to appreciate the things I learn that move me a step closer to Your purpose for my life. Help me to see change as a positive thing and to be patient in the process of all that must be.

May all who seek Your hands upon their lives find You. May they know Your love as You sculpt them into being and refine them in special ways to reflect Your light. *Amen.*

Rest in the Lord; wait patiently for Him. In Hebrew,
"Be silent in God, and let Him mold thee."
Keep still, and He will mold thee in the right shape.
~ Martin Luther ~

September 21

Give Me a Spark

A tiny spark can set a great forest on fire.
~ James 3:5 ~

Father, bless the spark that You have placed within me, that little divine light of love. Help me to reflect You because of all You have done for me and to share my joy with others.

I pray that my little spark would kindle a flame in the hearts of those who are part of my life. I pray that Your light would glow in my children and my family, my friends, and all who hear Your call.

Help me to feed the embers of Your love with continual attention to prayer and to reading Your Word. Help my flame to grow and show itself to others in a way that reflects Your glory. I ask that You would always bless me with a spark, a light, to shine for others. *Amen.*

Spirit-filled souls are ablaze for God. They love with a love that glows. They serve with a faith that kindles. They serve with a devotion that consumes.
~ Samuel Chadwick ~

September 22

The Favor of Flavor

"You are the salt of the earth. But what good is salt if it has lost its flavor?"

~ Matthew 5:13 ~

Lord, I thank You for being the salt within me, the One who makes my life worthwhile. I ask Your favor on my work, that I might flavor every task with Your grace and goodness. Help me to see my purpose in this world as being the "salt of the earth."

I pray, too, for those in leadership, or those who teach others, that they would be influenced by Your Spirit, grounded in faith, and working for the good of all people. I pray that we would all seek more of You and that any part of Your Spirit that exists within us would never be lost. I pray that we would never lose our flavor, our taste for all that You offer us.

Guard us with Your shield, raise us up with Your hope, and keep us ever faithful so we can find favor with You, and flavor the lives of those around us with Your Spirit. *Amen.*

May Your blessing be on Your people.

~ Psalm 3:8 NIV ~

Trust Issues

Our hope is in the living God, who is the Savior of all people.

~ 1 Timothy 4:10 ~

Lord, I confess that the world makes it tough to try to trust others. We often hope we can count on someone or that we can trust them, and then we discover that they have not honored us and that trust falls apart.

We try to trust the people we love, giving them our love and support, only to be grieved by broken trust when we least expect it.

Lord, I want to thank You that no matter what our earthly experiences are, we can at all times and in all ways trust You. I thank You that You are steadfast and faithful, and that we can rightly place our hope in You. Even when I don't understand, I know I can trust You to seek my good and to bring me comfort. *Amen.*

In God alone there is faithfulness, and faith in the trust that we may hold to Him, to His promise and to His guidance. To hold to God is to rely on the fact that God is there for me, and to live in this certainty.

~ Karl Barth ~

September 24

Producing Fruit

The Holy Spirit produces love, joy, peace, patience, kindness, goodness, faithfulness, gentleness, and self-control.

~ Galatians 5:22-23 ~

Lord, at this harvest time of year, I can only hope to be produce fruit that honors You and brings glory to Your name. I pray that Your Spirit would continue to help me grow in ways that make me more aware of the needs of others, and offer them kindness and respecte. I pray that my work would find favor and that, with patience and self-control, I may have opportunities to share Your light.

Bless all who seek to grow in faithfulness and joy. Bless the benefactors who give so graciously of their time and resources for the good of others. Grant that each day, more of Your children would produce the fruit of Your Spirit and demonstrate Your unending goodness to those around them. *Amen.*

It is the laden bough that hangs low, and the most fruitful Christian who is the most humble.

~ Anonymous ~

Thank God for Friends

A friend is always loyal, and a brother is born to help in time of need.

~ Proverbs 17:17 ~

Lord, what a generous gift it is to have true friends. Thank You for the people who make life more meaningful, the ones who hear our concerns, comfort our sadness, and applaud our achievements.

Thank You for the people who allow us to be ourselves and who accept us as we are without feeling a need to fix us or change us into someone else.

I pray for each of my friends and ask Your blessing on their lives. I pray that You would keep them safe from harm, grant them good health, and provide for their needs. I pray that whatever needs they may have today, that You would be near to help them. I offer thanks and praise for all my friendships. *Amen.*

There is no wilderness like a life without friends; friendship multiplies blessings and minimizes misfortunes; it is a unique remedy against adversity, and it soothes the soul.

~ Baltasar Gracian ~

Foolish Me!

You must make allowance for each other's faults, and forgive the person who offends you.
~ Colossians 3:13 ~

Lord, I am often perplexed about my own behavior, especially when I do those foolish things I know I'll regret later. I thank You for people who forgive me when I'm irritable or barely reasonable. I thank You for the many times You've helped me get back on track. I thank You even more that You bear with my outrageous behavior, the sins that would weigh me down if it weren't for You.

Bless all those who seek to change the things they do that are simply foolish. Grant us greater wisdom. Help us to seek Your face, Your Word, and Your guidance, so we may be re-clothed in You, O Lord. *Amen.*

Dear Lord and Father of mankind,
Forgive our foolish ways!
Re-clothe us in our rightful mind,
In purer lives Thy service find,
In deeper reverence, praise.
~ John Greenleaf Whittier ~

September 27

Prayer Works!

Seek the LORD while you can find Him. Call on Him now while He is near. Let the people turn from their wicked deeds. Let them banish from their minds the very thought of doing wrong.
~ Isaiah 55:6-7 ~

Lord, I understand that for the gift of prayer to work, I have to be more intentional about spending time in prayer. I know that the only way I can hear Your voice is if I quiet myself and let go of the constant noise of the world. You can only help me if I call Your name.

Father, thank You for being available to me whenever I call. Thank You for walking with me through the day. Guide me into Your truth, that I might give up the foolish thoughts that go through my mind. Help me to be awake to You in every way and in all things. Forgive my blindness and lead me always toward Your light. *Amen.*

I love the LORD, for He heard my voice;
He heard my cry for mercy. Because He turned
His ear to me, I will call on Him as long as I live.
~ Psalm 116:1-2 NIV ~

September 28

Just by Chance

I have observed something else in this world of ours. The fastest runner doesn't always win the race, and the strongest warrior doesn't always win the battle.
~ *Ecclesiastes 9:11* ~

Father, I prefer to think that our lives are not left simply to chance, but that You are ever watchful and aware of all that happens to Your children.

I ask that You would orchestrate things in our lives so that what may seem to us to be a case of being in the right place at the right time will truly be a case of divine intervention. Be with us as we learn to take a chance now and then, as we learn to trust You. Lead us in such a way that all outcomes will be those that were already planned and prepared by You. *Amen.*

I am glad there is no such thing as chance,
that nothing is left to itself, but that
Christ everywhere has sway.
~ *Charles H. Spurgeon* ~

What Motivates You?

"The human heart is the most deceitful of all things and desperately wicked. I, the LORD, search all hearts and examine secret motives."

~ Jeremiah 17:9-10 ~

Lord, I am so grateful that You know me so well. I thank You for being willing to search my heart and to seek those things in me that are good. Help me to always be motivated by things that bring hope and light and life to others. Help me to be motivated to bless the lives of those around me and to seek whatever good deeds I might do on any given day.

Bless everyone who seeks Your voice and needs Your guidance to do work that will please You. Bless each person and encourage each soul that desires to serve You with a pure heart. *Amen.*

I am only one, but still I am one.
I cannot do everything, but still I can do something;
And because I cannot do everything
I will not refuse to do the something that I can do.

~ Edward Everett Hale ~

Grant that I may not pray alone
with the mouth;
Help me that I may pray
from the depths of my heart.

~ Martin Luther ~

October

An Adventurous Spirit

For since the world began, no ear has heard, and no eye has seen a God like You, who works for those who wait for Him! You welcome those who cheerfully do good, who follow godly ways.

~ Isaiah 64:4-5 ~

Lord, if there's anything I've learned on my life journey, it's that everything is an adventure with You. I believe that the greatest joy on this earth is the opportunity You give us to walk the path in Your presence, to do the work You have ordained for us.

Today, Father, I pray for all who seek a new path, who blaze a trail where no one has been before. I thank You for the voices that echo Your name all over the world, offering Your hope and Your love to those who may have never heard it before.

Help me be willing to set out with the heart of an adventurer and create a new path to Your door for at least one more person. In Jesus' name. *Amen.*

Do not go where the path may lead; go instead where there is no path and leave a trail.

~ Ralph Waldo Emerson ~

Specially Chosen

"'I will treat you like a signet ring on My finger,' says the LORD, 'for I have specially chosen you. I, the LORD Almighty, have spoken!'"

~ Haggai 2:23 ~

Lord, I am so grateful that You chose me and loved me before I chose and loved You. I'm humbled that You would find anything in me that is worthy of Your mercy and grace. I try to imagine what it might mean for You to actually keep me close to You, perhaps like a beautiful ring worn with joy and pride, signifying something important and special. I know that You see each one of Your children as unique and special.

It's humbling to even think about. I praise You for Your incredible kindness to me. You do not wait for me to be perfect, You simply walk with me and offer me Your coaching and guidance. Thank You for treating me in such a special way. *Amen.*

For the LORD takes delight in His people; He crowns the humble with salvation. Let the saints rejoice in this honor and sing for joy on their beds.

~ Psalm 149:4-5 NIV ~

October 2

Believing and Receiving

To all who believed Him and accepted Him, He gave the right to become children of God. They are reborn!
~ John 1:12-13 ~

Dear Father of all, Creator of this world, You defy definition because You are all things and without You, there is simply nothing worth measuring. You lure us in with Your unending love and faithfulness. You teach us when we ask for guidance, carry us when we stumble, and forgive us when we do unspeakable things.

Lord, You are beyond our comprehension, yet so easy to see when we look for You. You keep us strong and shape us according to Your will and Your purpose. How humbled we are by Your blessings.

Lord, watch over all Your children, blessing their lives with Your holy touch, and Your loving Spirit.

Amen.

Great is our Lord and mighty in power;
His understanding has no limit.
The LORD sustains the humble.
~ Psalm 147:5-6 NIV ~

Fall Down, and Get Up!

If you think you are standing strong, be careful, for you, too, may fall into the same sin.
~ 1 Corinthians 10:12 ~

Lord, I know that I am always standing in the need of prayer. I'm reluctant to think about how easily I can be drawn off into areas of life that do not serve You or me very well.

This world is full of snares and temptations and many of us fall down over and over again. We need You to help us get back on our feet, get closer to You, and start again to walk in Your ways. Forgive us when we neglect You and when we simply walk in the wrong direction.

I ask that You would be with those today who have a desire in their hearts to come back to You, to get up again and follow Your path. Help all of us, Father, because of Your dear Son. *Amen.*

Because I love Your commands more than gold, more than pure gold, and because I consider all Your precepts right, I hate every wrong path.
~ Psalm 119:127-128 NIV ~

October 4

Shuffling the Deck

I want you to do whatever will help you serve the Lord
best, with as few distractions as possible.
~ *1 Corinthians 7:35* ~

Lord, I know better than to get too comfortable. My life experience tells me that the way I work best with You and for You is when I'm slightly off center, somewhat uncomfortable. I know that You often have to shuffle the deck and deal me a new hand.

It's good to know that even though it's the same deck, there's a new opportunity each time a hand is dealt. I want to serve You in every possible way and when You deal me another hand, I see a new possibility.

Thank You for making me take new steps and for helping me overcome fears that change often brings. Thank You for going ahead of me and preparing the way in each thing I do. *Amen.*

I will walk about in freedom,
for I have sought out Your precepts.
~ *Psalm 119:45 NIV* ~

October 5

Finding the Light

Who among you fears the Lord and obeys His servant?
If you are walking in darkness, without a ray of light,
trust in the Lord and rely on your God. But watch
out, you who live in your own light and warm your-
selves by your own fires.
~ Isaiah 50:10-11 ~

Father of light, grant that we might be lifted out of
the darkness that we see all around us, and add Your
light to our steps.

I pray especially for those who are still in darkness, who do not even know that they are asleep. I
pray that they may be illuminated by Your presence
in their lives and see Your hand at work. I pray that
they would embrace You with all their hearts and
minds and souls. Wake them up, Lord!

Please be near so that when we stumble in the
darkness, we can still hear Your voice and be led
back to the light of Your love. *Amen.*

Open my eyes that I may see
wonderful things in Your law.
~ Psalm 119:18 NIV ~

October 6

No Cowards Here

When I had lost all hope, I turned my thoughts once more to the LORD.

~ Jonah 2:7 ~

Father, You bring the hope to each day and the possibility to each life event. You bring the reason to continue to fight for the good, and win or lose, You echo the joy that helps us do it all over again on a new day.

Thank You for being with us as we learn and grow and manage what this world gives us. Sometimes it brings the victory that we can feel and taste and see. Other times, it covers us with a darkness that makes us wonder if we'll see Your face ever again.

Be with those who turn their thoughts to You today. Bless their lives and give them the victory found only in You. *Amen.*

Be strong and take heart,
all you who hope in the LORD.
~ Psalm 31:24 *NIV* ~

Of Snakes and Miracles

Then the Lord told him, "Make a replica of a poisonous snake and attach it to the top of a pole. Those who are bitten will live if they simply look at it!"
~ Numbers 21:8 ~

Lord, in a culture filled with technological advances, and cures for diseases that never existed before, we lose sight of the miraculous. We forget that none of those advances in medicine or science happened without Your inspiration and direction.

As hard as it is for us to imagine that the people of Israel were healed when they simply looked at the image of a bronze serpent, we know that nothing is impossible for You. Thank You for Your willingness to manifest opportunities for us to see Your hand at work even through the use of miracles.

Help us to trust You for all the details of our lives. You know when we need healing and when we need to receive water from a stone. *Amen.*

Glorify the Lord with me;
let us exalt His name together.
~ Psalm 34:3 NIV ~

October 8

Send Me, Send Me!

*Then I heard the Lord asking, "Whom should I send as
a messenger to My people? Who will go for us?" And
I said, "Lord, I'll go! Send me."*
~ Isaiah 6:8 ~

Lord, it is an honor to serve You. I pray that whatever
part I might play in furthering Your work that You
would find me available when You call. I pray that
my heart would be fully submissive and ready to
answer, "Send me, send me!"

Thank You for the opportunities You've given
me already to shine Your light. Whether I work as a
flashlight or a beacon, I am humbled by the chance
to do so. Help me to stand strong for You, faithful in
my work and calling, and always ready to be Your
messenger. Bless all who speak in Your name and
shed Your light on others. *Amen.*

*Praise be to the LORD, for He
showed His wonderful love to me.*
~ Psalm 31:21 *NIV* ~

All in the Family

"Anyone who does the will of My Father in heaven is My brother and sister and mother!"
~ Matthew 12:50 ~

Lord, with You as our Father, we are all family. We are the human family and what affects one of us, affects all of us. Help us to grasp the fact that we are part of You and in that way we are meant to help each other grow and be strong.

Forgive us when we don't treat other members of our family well. Forgive our stubborn hearts and our meanness of spirit against those who think differently, live differently, or even believe differently than we do. Help us to feel Your presence in the light of all the people we meet. Help us to embrace each other and never leave anyone feeling like a stranger.

Guide us to be gracious siblings, kindly parents, and blessed family members to each other. *Amen.*

Earthly fathers and mothers, husbands, wives, children, or the company of earthly friends, are but shadows. But the enjoyment of God is the substance.
~ Jonathan Edwards ~

October 10

Knowing the Rules

Jesus replied, "'You must love the Lord your God with all your heart, all your soul, and all your mind.' And 'Love your neighbor as yourself.'"
~ Matthew 22:37, 39 ~

Lord, we have managed to make millions of rules, and have cluttered up the two basic rules You gave us for living well. We have piled our own interpretations upon Your two rules and built walls around ourselves that are padded with uncertainty.

Today, Lord, I ask that You would lead us with a clear vision of Your rules. Teach us to love God and each other with authentic hearts. Help us to encourage each other and bring light to the soul. Grant us Your blessings as we learn to more fully appreciate and honor Your rules for us. *Amen.*

The law of the Lord is perfect, reviving the soul.
The statutes of the Lord are trustworthy,
making wise the simple.
~ Psalm 19:7 NIV ~

Plugged In

*"This is the plan determined for the whole world; this is the hand stretched out over all nations. For the L*ORD *Almighty has purposed and who can thwart Him?"*
~ Isaiah 14:26-27 ~

Lord, if I try to imagine just what it truly means to plug into the God of the Universe, the Creator of all things, I can't do it. I can't conceive of the kind of love that comes to earth in the form of a baby simply to give me a loving way to return to heaven one day. I can't conceive of the power that forms planets and mountains and human beings out of the dust of the ground. But, Lord, even though my imagination is sorely limited, my heart has had a glimpse of Your light. My soul has mustard-seed faith and I long to always be connected to You, the only living Source of all that is good. Help me to embrace Your love and Your power in my life. *Amen.*

*Exalt the L*ORD *our God and worship at His holy mountain, for the L*ORD *our God is holy.*
~ Psalm 99:9 NIV ~

October 12

Gracious Giving

"Give to those who ask, and don't turn away from those who want to borrow."
~ Matthew 5:42 ~

Lord, I pray today for those who have been hurt by life in such a way that they now find themselves to be homeless. I pray that whatever their circumstances might be that You would come to them, sending people into their lives who can help them.

The numbers of people in need around the globe increase by the hour and it becomes overwhelming to understand how to help them all, how to ease the suffering of even a few. I ask for Your guidance in knowing where to put what little I am able to give to their needs.

I surrender my resources to You and ask that You would bless them, helping me to use them wisely and well for my family and for others. *Amen.*

Good will come to him who is generous and lends freely, who conducts affairs with justice.
~ Psalm 112:5 NIV ~

October 13

Understanding God

"O Father, Lord of heaven and earth, thank You for hiding the truth from those who think themselves to be wise and clever, and for revealing it to the childlike."
~ Matthew 11:25 ~

Father, I am awed that You found a way to make it easy for us to receive You. I thank You for the gift of childlike faith that drinks in all that You have to offer without question. Help us to seek You with our hearts. I pray for all who seek to understand more of Your ways. I ask that You would pour Your Holy Spirit out on those who desire more of You so that they may grow and learn and prosper according to Your will and plan for their lives.

Forgive us when we lose faith. Help us to desire more of Your wisdom. Thank You for loving us in spite of our sinful ways. *Amen.*

*The Lord upholds all those who fall
and lifts up all who are bowed down.*
~ Psalm 145:14 NIV ~

October 14

Finding Level Ground

Do not stifle the Holy Spirit. Do not scoff at prophecies, but test everything that is said. Hold on to what is good. Keep away from every kind of evil.
~ 1 Thessalonians 5:19-22 ~

Lord, how guilty I am of believing that I can handle life on my own without bringing all things to Your throne. Forgive my foolishness and lead me back to Yourself that I would know Your will for me and give the glory to You.

Bless the people on this earth who look to You to put them on level ground, who hope in Your mercy and Your provision.

Help all of us to hold on to what is good and not be overcome by the temptations of this world. Help us to flee from things that will not serve You and will only deprive us of Your peace. *Amen.*

Teach me to do Your will, for You are my God;
may Your good Spirit lead me on level ground.
~ Psalm 143:10 NIV ~

Following Noah!

My heart says of You, "Seek His face!" Your face,
Lord, I will seek.

~ Psalm 27:8 NIV ~

Lord, I sometimes wonder if the earth itself is not a form of the ark. You have been sending messages to us over and over again to prepare for Your coming. You've given us lots of time to make choices before You finally close the door. I ask that You would create a desire in all Your children to prepare for You and to get ready for all that is to come.

Help us be willing to tell others so that we can bring as many into the ark of Your love as possible. Grant us mercy and grace to hear Your calling. I pray for all who have not had ears to hear or eyes to see, that they would indeed hear Your voice today. *Amen.*

You have been once more warned today,
while the door of the ark yet stands open.
You have, as it were, once again heard the knocks
of the hammer and axe in the building of the ark,
to put you in mind that a flood is approaching.

~ Jonathan Edwards ~

Worry Warts

"I am leaving you with a gift – peace of mind and heart. And the peace I give isn't like the peace the world gives. So don't be troubled or afraid."
~ *John 14:27* ~

Lord, help me to get past my fears and worries and keep my eyes looking heavenward. Help me to trust in You no matter what circumstances befall me here. Keep me in Your peace and let me embrace the gift of that peace each day.

The world is a troubled place and surely the devil finds it easy to frighten us even further with his lies and temptations. For each person today who is troubled or worried, Lord, I claim victory over that worry in the name of Jesus. I claim that all who stand on Your promises are set free because of Your love and faithfulness. Release us from the grip of worry and hold us tenderly to Yourself. *Amen.*

The troubles of my heart have multiplied;
free me from my anguish.
~ *Psalm 25:17 NIV* ~

Getting Things Done

Joshua did as he was told, carefully obeying all of the LORD's instructions to Moses.
~ Joshua 11:15 ~

Lord, most of us set up to-do lists. We have goals to achieve at work or at home or in the growth of a relationship, but sometimes we forget to look at our to-do list from You.

Help me today to look for Your desire for my life. Open my eyes to see what You would have me do and help me to execute those plans. Forgive me when I put Your will aside and go my own way. I know that nothing brings me greater joy than actually doing something that will please You. We may not always be obedient and for those times when we're not, forgive us. For those times when we are, bless us and help us to grow more aware of Your will. You brought each of us here for a purpose and nothing will make our lives feel sweeter than achieving Your goals. *Amen.*

All the ways of the LORD are loving and faithful for those who keep the demands of His covenant.
~ Psalm 25:10 NIV ~

October 18

Doing What's Right

God gives wisdom, knowledge, and joy to those who please Him.

~ Ecclesiastes 2:26 ~

Lord, most of us try to do the right thing. You have given us a strong moral compass and we know that when we're willing to be guided by it, our lives are more peaceful and we're filled with contentment.

Sometimes knowing what's right isn't simple to understand. Sometimes we have to make the hard choices and lean in closer to You to determine our direction. Those times can be a little scary and test our faith.

Lord, today, I pray for all the people on this planet who strive to do the right thing, to act with kindness and love toward others, and to listen more attentively to Your voice. Help all of us to live with a busy, active faith and do those things that please You. *Amen.*

Faith is a living, busy, active, powerful thing! It is impossible for it not to do us good continually.
~ Martin Luther ~

October 19

It Doesn't Make Sense

All that I know now is partial and incomplete, but then I will know everything completely, just as God knows me now.

~ 1 Corinthians 13:12 ~

Lord, often times the world seems upside down. Criminals are set free, and victims go unheard. Families dissolve, and children get hurt. People of faith are ridiculed and people without mercy rise to power. It's so hard to understand and it doesn't make sense.

I know that we only have a piece of the picture now. We cannot see from Your vantage point exactly how things come together. That's why we need to walk in faith. That's the reason we come to You on our knees and ask You to watch out for us. Lord, bless Your children, the weak ones and the strong ones. Most of all, Father, I pray that You would continue to enlighten us, granting us greater wisdom and the ability to see those things You would have us know. *Amen.*

Give me understanding, and I will keep
Your law and obey it with all my heart.
~ Psalm 119:34 NIV ~

October 20

When Sorrow Calls

When I heard this, I sat down and wept. In fact, for days I mourned, fasted, and prayed to the God of heaven.

~ *Nehemiah 1:4* ~

Lord, we are burdened by grief. We weep for innocent children who are hurt each day by lost and angry adults. We grieve for families in turmoil, heartbroken for members of their households who are paralyzed by life and confused about their direction.

We find loss waiting on every corner. Sometimes it's the death of someone we love. Sometimes it's a job that came to an end. Sometimes it's a relationship that shattered between our fingers. For all these times, and others too numerous to name, I ask Your help. I ask that You would protect innocent children, bind the wounds of the broken in spirit, and grant mercy to those who have lost their way. We look to You for hope and guidance. *Amen.*

*He heals the brokenhearted and
binds up their wounds.*
~ *Psalm 147:3* NIV ~

Good News

Good news from far away is like cold water to the thirsty.

~ Proverbs 25:25 ~

Lord, thank You for giving us the opportunity to grasp the Good News. In fact, much of the time, we don't really realize how lost we are without You.

Your goodness and grace and mercy are amazing and wonderful, but the truth is, we don't really fully understand it all. We live on a planet that makes a lot of things hard, and everywhere we look, it seems like the villains are winning.

Help us to stop all the noise from the outside world. Help us to seek the Good News only You can give us and help us to wake up to the important matters of faith. *Amen.*

How good it is to sing praises to our God, how pleasant and fitting to praise Him!

~ Psalm 147:1 NIV ~

Keeping Out of Danger

"Keep alert and pray. Otherwise temptation will over-power you. For though the spirit is willing enough, the body is weak!"

~ Matthew 26:41 ~

Father, when You taught us to pray, You reminded us that we need to always be mindful of not being led into temptation. The difficult part is that temptation seems to jump into our paths all the time. If we're trying to lose weight, all we can think about is food and every commercial makes us feel hungry.

Help us! Help those who struggle with addictions to things that are shortening their lives, costing them friendships and causing hardships. I pray for all those who seek Your help with any kind of temptation. "Lead us not into temptation and deliver us from evil." *Amen.*

Forgive my hidden faults. Keep Your servant also from willful sins; may they not rule over me.
~ Psalm 19:12-13 NIV ~

October 23

Be Still!

*For this is the secret: Christ lives in you, and this is
your assurance that you will share in His glory.*
~ Colossians 1:27 ~

Lord, grant that we might find You in the stillness
today. Help us to quiet our minds and hearts in
such a way that we will see more of Your Spirit in all
things. Help us to choose the way that allows You to
enter in and open the door a bit wider for us to see
You more clearly.

Thank You for living within us, for always being
a simple thought away, a brief prayer, a moment of
gentle connection. We long to know You. We long to
find You in the midst of this life, for You are the one
certainty that we can attain.

The only thing that matters is joining You in that
space where we quietly find You any time we call.

Amen.

*"Be still, and know that I am God; I will be exalted
among the nations, I will be exalted in the earth."*
~ Psalm 46:10 NIV ~

October 24

What Happened to Security?

You will see Jerusalem, a city quiet and secure. The LORD will be our Mighty One. He will be like a wide river of protection that no enemy can cross.
~ Isaiah 33:20-21 ~

Father, many people live hand to mouth, day to day, with no real sense of security. Their homes are not safe, their finances are all but gone, and their families are set against each other. We are people with no sense of security apart from You. Only in You can we have a place to rest. Only at Your feet can we receive comfort and assurance.

Bless those who look to You. Bless those who have lost any sense of what it means to be secure and remind them that in You, they are well. In You, they have hope. In You, is the only security that can ever be found. *Amen.*

"My hand will sustain him;
surely My arm will strengthen him."
~ Psalm 89:21 NIV ~

Let Your Conscience Be Your Guide

I have always lived before God in all good conscience!
~ Acts 23:1 ~

Lord, You've given us a way to determine right from wrong, good choices from bad ones. You've placed a level of Your Holy Spirit within us to guide us and we often call it conscience.

I pray, Lord, that Your voice would ring loud and clear to all those who are in positions of leadership and authority. I pray for teachers and parents and those who mold and shape children around the world, that their sense of You would be strong and that they would have a good conscience about the things they do.

I pray that those who wish to let their conscience be their guide would know that it is Your truth and Your Spirit that truly seeks to guide their way. *Amen.*

He who dwells in the shelter of the Most High
will rest in the shadow of the Almighty.
~ Psalm 91:1 NIV ~

October 26

It's Good for the Soul

*But if we confess our sins to Him, He is faithful and
just to forgive us and to cleanse us from every wrong.*
~ 1 John 1:9 ~

Lord, thank You for giving us a way to confess those
things that bring us shame. Forgive those things that
we cannot even understand about ourselves; choices
we made that we knew would be foolish, sins we
committed knowingly, and sins of omission because
we didn't want to take the time to do the right thing.

We know that only the truth can set us free and
so we share our sin with You, knowing that You will
forgive us. Grant us the freedom to try again, to do
better next time. We come to You now with contrite
hearts knowing that on our own, we cannot move
past our own sinfulness. Only You can set us free
and that's what we ask in Jesus' name. *Amen.*

*Judgment will again be founded on righteousness,
and all the upright in heart will follow it.*
~ Psalm 94:15 NIV ~

Wise Words

*Teach us to number our days aright, that we may gain
a heart of wisdom.*

~ Psalm 90:12 NIV ~

Lord, we are so good at patting ourselves on the back
when we do even one small thing that seems good
or brilliant in our own eyes. We're good at giving
ourselves credit even when any good deed we may
have done could only happen because of the gifts
You provided to make it all possible.

We lack wisdom! Help us to be wise in all that we
do, according to Your ways. Help us to want to know
more of Your nature and Your purpose so that our
choices are ones made with wisdom.

Bless us with enough of a foolish heart that we
long to fall at Your feet of grace and to then soak up
all we can of Your Spirit. Help us want to be wiser in
Your eyes. Nothing else really matters. *Amen.*

*We are ensnared by the wisdom of the serpent;
we are set free by the foolishness of God.*

~ St. Augustine ~

October 28

A Little More Patience

We can rejoice, too, when we run into problems and trials, for we know that they are good for us – they help us learn to endure. And endurance develops strength of character in us, and character strengthens our confident expectation of salvation.

~ Romans 5:3-4 ~

Lord, it's not easy to be patient. Sometimes it feels like the more patient we try to become, the more we have to endure. Help us not to think that we could somehow create better circumstances more quickly ourselves.

Help us to see the errors of our thinking when we become less willing to wait, impatient and impulsive, and coming only to a place that lacks peace and joy. Forgive those choices we make out of a need to take care of things ourselves because we simply couldn't wait any longer. Help all of us to endure our problems and place all our trust in You. *Amen.*

Wait for the Lord; be strong and take heart and wait for the Lord.
~ Psalm 27:14 *niv* ~

October 29

Simple Gifts

If your gift is that of serving others, serve them well. If you are a teacher, do a good job of teaching. If your gift is to encourage others, do it! If you have money, share it generously. If God has given you leadership ability, take the responsibility seriously. And if you have a gift for showing kindness to others, do it gladly.

~ Romans 12:7-8 ~

Lord, You have been so generous to us. You have given us great gifts to share with each other, making it possible for us to help each other through all of life's events. Help us to remember to share our gifts with joy and with reckless abandon as though we can't get enough of giving all we have to others.

Bless those who use their gifts wisely and well, and encourage them to keep doing so. Inspire us to always seek ways to use the gifts You've given us.

Amen.

Nothing is small if God accepts it.
~ St. Teresa of Ávila ~

October 30

Time for the Harvest

"As long as the earth remains, there will be springtime and harvest, cold and heat, winter and summer, day and night."

~ Genesis 8:22 ~

Lord, we celebrate the harvest, the opportunity to partake of the things we have planted. We thank You for being the Lord of the harvest, the One who graciously watered our crops to make them grow and blessed us with abundance.

Any time we have the chance to see the fruit of our labors, Lord, help us to be generous in sharing that fruit with others. Enrich the ones who plant seeds of grace and who offer the generous waters of joy to bless our lives as we grow.

Bless people all around the world who have planted their seeds of hope, prayed for Your grace, and await the bounty of their efforts. *Amen.*

Blessed are all who fear the LORD, and walk in His ways. You will eat the fruit of your labor; blessings and prosperity will be yours.
~ Psalm 128:1-2 NIV ~

October 31

The Serenity Prayer

God, give me Grace to accept with serenity
the things that cannot be changed,
Courage to change the things
which should be changed,
and the Wisdom to distinguish
the one from the other.

~ Reinhold Niebuhr ~

November

Learning Curves

Teach the wise, and they will be wiser. Teach the righteous, and they will learn more.
~ Proverbs 9:9 ~

Lord, we usually think that trying something new comes with a learning curve. We need time to grasp a new concept or the culture of a new workplace. Perhaps in life, though, the real learning curve comes each time we have to get past our own egos. We have to "unlearn" those things we thought were right and look again.

Help me be willing to look at all the areas of my life with a fresh perspective. Where have I gotten stale, doing things the same way I've always done them?

Help me and help others too who want to know the truth and who are willing to learn new things. Help us to embrace the learning curves and to welcome the challenge they bring. *Amen.*

It is what we think we know already that often prevents us from learning.
~ Claude Bernard ~

Choosing the Light

Choose today whom you will serve.
~ Joshua 24:15 ~

Father, I don't always think about it, but I know that each day, and each hour of the day, I make choices. I choose to either serve You or serve myself. Serving myself seldom gives me joy or satisfaction.

This life is short and it is important for us to embrace Your light in every possible way. Please walk with us in the light and help us to stay out of the darkness. The darkness lurks everywhere seeking to change our direction and claim some aspect of our being.

Bless each person who comes humbly to You, seeking more understanding and illumination. Reach out to them and teach them Your ways. Help them to share that light with others and to seek to grow in faith. *Amen.*

The issue now is clear. It is between light and darkness and everyone must choose his side.
~ G. K. Chesterton ~

November 2

Life Lessons

"The thief's purpose is to steal and kill and destroy.
My purpose is to give life in all its fullness."
~ John 10:10 ~

Lord, all of us are sinners and so we do not manage our time well. We don't manage our home life well either, for we always think we'll have another day to spend with our children, or another moment to share a board game or read a book together. Sometimes, though, a thief comes in the night and destroys all that we might hope for and reminds us that life passes quickly, so we must educate ourselves to learn all we can.

Grant that we might understand our purpose for being born so that we might honor You in all things. Help us to grasp as many life lessons as we possibly can and use them wisely. Help us to learn more about how to love others. *Amen.*

As for man, his days are like grass, he flourishes
like a flower of the field; the wind blows over it and
it is gone, and its place remembers it no more.
~ Psalm 103:15-16 NIV ~

A Life of Faith

What is faith? It is the confident assurance that what we hope for is going to happen. It is the evidence of things we cannot yet see.

~ Hebrews 11:1 ~

Lord, bless all those who strive to live a life of faith. Bless them so that they have genuine peace and don't have a care in the world. Take their cares and let them slip away as You show the ways that trusting in You can make a difference.

Help all of us to trust You past what our eyes can see, beyond what our ears can hear, and over any cares that come our way. Help us to live a life of genuine faith … standing on the rock of Jesus for all we do. *Amen.*

For as high as the heavens are above the earth, so great is His love for those who fear Him.
~ Psalm 103:11 NIV ~

November 4

Hope and Love

I wait for the Lord, my soul waits, and in His word I put my hope.

~ Psalm 130:5 NIV ~

Lord, help me to grow up in matters of faith. Sometimes I feel like a child, hoping when nothing seems possible, wondering how to have the kind of faith that makes a difference. I look to You and seek Your face to help me become more aware, more understanding of the things You would have me know.

I pray to be a person of great faith and in that faith to make a difference in the lives of those around me. I pray to demonstrate Your love by the work of my hands, the words of my mouth, and the choices I make. I ask You today to help me become stronger in hope and in love.

Help me to put my hope in the right things so that I can place them humbly in Your hands. *Amen.*

There is no love without hope, no hope without love, and neither hope nor love without faith.

~ St. Augustine ~

Innocent Suffering

Everything is pure to those whose hearts are pure. But nothing is pure to those who are corrupt and unbelieving, because their minds and consciences are defiled.

~ Titus 1:15 ~

Lord, it happened again today … another newspaper account of innocent children gunned down at a school for no apparent reason. Many children were killed before the insanity was stopped as the gunman shot himself. Now the suffering remains for everyone, even those of us who are not close by.

Help us to prevent tragedies like this one. Comfort those poor children who are traumatized by witnessing such an event in their young lives. Help all the people involved in this sad experience, and help all of us to seek You with our whole hearts to keep these dark events away. *Amen.*

Taking us through suffering, not out of it,
is one of the primary means that the
Spirit uses today in bringing us to God.
~ Daniel Wallace ~

November 6

Reward Poster

Be strong and courageous, for your work will be rewarded.

~ 2 Chronicles 15:7 ~

Lord, I guess all of us who hope for heaven are goal seekers. After all, we are anxiously awaiting a crown and a chance to reap the rewards of being faithful.

We do put our hope in You, Lord, but we realize that nothing we do can actually be worthy of a reward. After all, Your Son paid a high price to redeem us and make it even possible for us to come home again to You. We thank You for Your faithfulness and for the mercy we can never earn or deserve.

Reward those who work so hard for You in this life. Grant them peace of mind and joy in their spirits. Help them to feel Your grace and comfort around them in all they do. Reward them, too, with the gift of Your presence each day. *Amen.*

When God crowns our merits,
He crowns nothing else but His own gifts.
~ St. Augustine ~

What Seems Reasonable?

*Your statutes are forever right; give me understanding
that I may live.*

~ Psalm 119:144 *NIV* ~

Lord, You have given us the gifts of reasoning so that
we could think through the things we do and work
to discover more of what You want us to understand.
We know that if we come to You, that together we
might be able to reason out some of what life is about.

Today, I pray for the ability to be more reasonable, especially in matters of the heart and matters
of divine grace and principles. Help me to seek Your
voice any time I'm trying to understand things that
do not yet seem reasonable to me. *Amen.*

*There is a difficulty about disagreeing with God.
He is the source from which all your
reasoning power comes.*

~ C. S. Lewis ~

Worth Reading

Great are the works of the LORD; they are pondered by all who delight in them.

~ Psalm 111:2 NIV ~

Lord, we have more information at our fingertips than any generation had before us. Help us to use our time wisely as we read, giving our minds the opportunity to explore and consider new ideas, new possibilities, and a new understanding of our life purpose.

Give us a greater desire to spend more time reading Your Word and becoming immersed in it in ways that strengthen us so we are prepared to tackle the really tough issues of life. Fill us with Your Holy Spirit so we can be discerning as we read, discovering Your voice in the pages. Thank You for the power of words to shape our hearts and minds, especially Your Word. *Amen.*

Seek in reading and you will find in meditation; knock in prayer and it will be opened to you in contemplation.

~ St. John of the Cross ~

Good Question!

"You can ask for anything in My name, and I will do it, because the work of the Son brings glory to the Father. Yes, ask anything in My name, and I will do it!"

~ John 14:13-14 ~

Father, thank You that we can bring all our questions to You. Thank You for receiving those questions and giving them careful consideration. Grant that we might realize that once we've asked for Your help, that we can be content knowing You are already working on the answers.

Forgive us the doubts that assail us when our questions seem to go unanswered. Help us to trust that You work all things together for our good and that You do not make mistakes. Thank You for hearing our questions and even our doubts. We place all that we are into Your hands. *Amen.*

Let them give thanks to the LORD for His unfailing love and His wonderful deeds for men, for He satisfies the thirsty and fills the hungry with good things.

~ Psalm 107:8-9 NIV ~

November 10

When I'm Prejudiced!

All who have been united with Christ in baptism have been made like Him. There is no longer Jew or Gentile, slave or free, male or female. For you are all Christians— you are one in Christ Jesus.

~ Galatians 3:27-28 ~

Lord, help me to see clearly those things that keep me bound to unfounded and unnecessary prejudices, stories that I've told myself, or that I somehow embraced as I was growing up, but stories that are simply not true.

Help me to see all people regardless of culture or creed as Your people. Help me to look for Jesus in each face I see and to offer the love of Christ to all people as my friends and neighbors. Help me to embrace the differences in each of us, but to realize we are more alike than different and that we all have the same Father. *Amen.*

We want the facts to fit the preconceptions. When they don't, it is easier to ignore the facts than to change the preconceptions.

~ Jessamyn West ~

November 11

Prayer Requests

Seek the LORD while you can find Him. Call on Him now while He is near.

~ Isaiah 55:6 ~

Lord, as often as I come to You in prayer, I recognize that I don't always come with the right attitude, or perhaps with the right understanding of our time together.

Help me to seek Your truth in prayer, to open my heart in an attitude of trust, believing in Your grace and mercy. Help me to see that all prayer is meant to bring us together, to give us a chance to build our relationship and to know each other more fully.

Forgive me when I contemplate the distance between us or put up walls that make it hard for me to hear Your voice. Help me and all people who come to You in prayer, to be connected to You in a real and loving way. Help each of us to desire time with You no matter what our life issues may be. Raise our souls from earth to heaven through prayer. *Amen.*

May the LORD grant all your requests.

~ Psalm 20:5 *NIV* ~

November 12

Turn Your Radio On

My dear brothers and sisters, be quick to listen, slow to speak.

~ *James 1:19* ~

Lord, it's fascinating to me how easy it is for us to tune You out on any given day. We get lost in our work, get busy with our to-do lists and somehow don't notice all the little ways You're trying to get our attention. You wake us up with a beautiful sunrise and bless us with simple pleasures to start our day, and yet we still don't hear You.

I pray for all Your children today that they would plug in to whatever device helps them hear Your voice, and walk with You all through the day. Help each one to know that You are in control and that Your voice can be heard at all times. Thank You for finding so many ways to draw near to us. *Amen.*

I love to think of nature as an unlimited broadcasting station, through which God speaks to us every hour, if we will only tune in.
~ *George Washington Carver* ~

November 13

Living in the Light

For though your hearts were once full of darkness, now you are full of light from the Lord, and your behavior should show it!

~ Ephesians 5:8 ~

Father of all light, thank You for allowing us to shine and to share what little we have of Your glow. Thank You for creating within each of us a space where that blessed light can shine and grow. We have so much to learn about being the light in this world. We walk into the darkness and strive to light the way for others to see You.

I pray today for all those who shine Your light. Help them to act in ways that would please You and that would serve others. May they be a beacon of Your love wherever they are and never cease to offer guidance to those who seek to find the way. *Amen.*

Let the light of Your face shine upon us, O Lord.
~ Psalm 4:6 NIV ~

November 14

Weighing Our Words

Let everything you say be good and helpful, so that your words will be an encouragement to those who hear them.

~ Ephesians 4:29 ~

Father, I pray for all of us who speak in Your name that we would be careful to weigh our words. Remind us that words have the power to create and that we can impact others for a very long time with the words we speak.

Remind those who care for children, to offer them encouragement and blessings. Give parents the strength to be wise in their actions and in the tone of their voices and help them to be kind in every way.

Remind husbands and wives to seek the good in each other, holding up a light of love and possibility as they converse and connect. Words can bring healing and light and I pray that all of us would be aware of shining that light on others. *Amen.*

Words must be weighed, not counted.
~ Polish Proverb ~

November 15

All Work, No Play!

Work hard and cheerfully at whatever you do, as though you were working for the Lord rather than for people.

~ Colossians 3:23 ~

Lord, I guess the idea of creating a life of balance is a modern notion. After all, generations before us worked from sun up to sun down and just believed it was the way of life. They developed a work ethic that is unmatched in our current culture.

Help us to work in a way that brings You glory, and then to appreciate our time to relax and rest as part of Your plan for our lives. You told us to rest on the Sabbath, knowing that we would need some time to simply relax and to have the opportunity to focus on You. Help us to honor both work times and play times so that we can truly live balanced lives, and sacred lives according to Your plans and purposes. *Amen.*

Work is the meat of life, pleasure the dessert.
~ Bertie Charles Forbes ~

November 16

Uniquely Designed

So remember this and keep it firmly in mind: The Lord is God both in heaven and on earth, and there is no other god!

~ *Deuteronomy 4:39* ~

Lord, knowing that there is only one God in heaven and on earth is a comfort to our souls. It is the foundation stone on which we stand and build our lives.

Thank You, that even as there is only one God, You have designed each of us in a unique way so that there is and ever will be only one person that is us. We are each uniquely designed by Your loving hand. You placed us in families so that we could learn and grow, and develop the skills and talents that become our livelihood and our imprint on the world.

Thank You for creating each one of us, and for loving us so much that You gave us Jesus to bring us safely back to You when this life is done. *Amen.*

I praise You because I am fearfully and wonderfully made; Your works are wonderful, I know that full well.

~ *Psalm 139:14 NIV* ~

November 17

The Invitation

The Spirit and the bride say, "Come." Let each one who hears them say, "Come." Let the thirsty ones come – anyone who wants to. Let them come and drink the water of life without charge.
~ Revelation 22:17 ~

Lord, invite us into the work of Your Spirit that we might engage it more fully. Help us to clean up the areas of our lives that we have not been able or willing to surrender to You. Grant that we would focus all of our attention on accepting Your invitation to draw closer to You so that You can lead and guide and save us.

May our example serve as a light to others who have not yet accepted Your invitation and may You place a desire deep within their hearts to know more of You and to walk in Your ways. In the name of Jesus, I ask this. *Amen.*

Search me, O God, and know my heart; test me and know my anxious thoughts. See if there is any offensive way in me, and lead me in the way everlasting.
~ Psalm 139:23-24 NIV ~

November 18

Our Daily Bread

"I am the living bread that came down out of heaven. Anyone who eats this bread will live forever; this bread is My flesh, offered so the world may live."

~ *John 6:51* ~

Lord, thank You for being our daily bread and for keeping us well fed on Your Word and in our prayers. Thank You for being salt and light, and the anointing oil that keeps us working and functioning well for You.

I pray for all people who have not yet tasted of Your goodness and power, to do so today. I pray for all those who once invited You in but have forgotten how sweet You are to their lives, to seek You again. I pray that all may know You and find the joy only You can bring to the heart. *Amen.*

The LORD is near to all who call on Him, to all who call on Him in truth. He fulfills the desires of those who fear Him; He hears their cry and saves them.

~ *Psalm 145:18-19 NIV* ~

Living Today!

Rejoice. Change your ways. Encourage each other. Live in harmony and peace. Then the God of love and peace will be with you.

~ 2 Corinthians 13:11 ~

Lord, most of us struggle with living in the present. We are suffocated by the sins of yesterday, the problems that are not yet resolved, the aches and pains of foolish choices. Sometimes we have such good memories of the past, we choose to stay stuck there because we're afraid to move on into the future.

If we have managed to shake the past, then the future beckons, often with a sense of foreboding. How will we find a new job? When will we find the right life partner? What will happen to our children? The future becomes such a big question mark that we lose sight of the one thing we do have for sure … today! Help all of us use today wisely and live it with joy because of our faith in You. *Amen.*

The Lord is good to all; He has compassion on all He has made.

~ Psalm 145:9 NIV ~

November 20

Always and Forever

I am convinced that nothing can ever separate us from His love. Death can't, and life can't. The angels can't, and the demons can't. Our fears for today, or worries about tomorrow, and even the power of hell can't keep God's love away.

~ Romans 8:38 ~

Lord, how easily we forget about Your love, Your real and abiding love for us. Knowing our own fears and worries, we imagine that we're just not worthy of Your love and Your divine presence in our lives. It is so comforting to know that in truth, nothing can separate us from You.

I ask, Father, that You would bless each person who seeks You with a weary and humble heart. Offer Your comfort and mercy. Help each person to put all their fears and worries at Your feet.

I thank You for loving us so much more than we can ever comprehend. *Amen.*

Great is the LORD and most worthy of praise;
His greatness no one can fathom.
~ Psalm 145:3 NIV ~

Stones for Bread

"You parents – if your children ask for a loaf of bread, do you give them a stone instead? Or if they ask for fish, do you give them a snake? Of course not! If you sinful people know how to give good gifts to your children, how much more will your heavenly Father give good gifts to those who ask Him?"

~ Matthew 7:9-11 ~

Lord, we all love the idea of a gift. We love giving gifts and we love receiving gifts. Usually, though, when we think about gift giving, we aren't remembering that everything we have, everything we get to enjoy, even our humble talents are all gifts from You.

Help us to enjoy what we have now. Grant that we may continue to offer others the best of the gifts we have to share, and then keep us always protected and blessed by Your great love. Thank You for giving us the true Bread of Life. *Amen.*

God's gifts put man's best dreams to shame.
~ Elizabeth Barrett Browning ~

November 22

That Golden Rule

"Do for others what you would like them to do for you. This is a summary of all that is taught in the law and the prophets."

~ Matthew 7:12 ~

Lord, forgive us when we neglect the opportunity to serve others, even in the smallest ways. Help us to treat each person we meet with respect and kindness.

Help us to see beyond our own worries or pains, so that we are willing to lend a hand at a moment's notice, or offer encouragement when it is most needed. Be our Source of light and love to all the people we meet each day.

Thank You for the people who have shown such kindness to me and help me to open my heart and mind to the needs of others wherever I may be today. Bless those who seek to do all that is right and fair as they pass through this world. *Amen.*

Blessed is he whose help is the God of Jacob,
whose hope is in the LORD his God,
the Maker of heaven and earth.
~ Psalm 146:5-6 NIV ~

Thankful Living!

*Always be joyful. Keep on praying. No matter what
happens, always be thankful, for this is God's will for
you who belong to Christ Jesus.*
~ 1 Thessalonians 5:16-18 ~

Lord, help us to "think" our thanks to You all the
time. Help us to go on being joyful, even when the
crisis of the day strives to take hold of our minds and
lead us away from You. Remind us that in all things,
we have You to hear our prayers and You to come to
our aid. We are not alone.

Let us then give thanks for everything we have …
good health, loving families, bread on the table,
friends, and hope for tomorrow. As we learn to think
with thanks in our hearts, help us to live in a way
that shows our gratitude. *Amen.*

*Gratitude is from the same root word as grace – the
boundless mercy of God. Thanksgiving is from the
same root word as think, so to think is to thank.*
~ Willis P. King ~

November 24

Irresistible Grace!

Now glory be to God! By His mighty power at work within us, He is able to accomplish infinitely more than we would ever dare to ask or hope.
~ Ephesians 3:20 ~

Father, there is more power and hope in Your acts of grace than I can even imagine or begin to comprehend. You have given each of us a taste of Your Divine Spirit, granting us wisdom and possibility according to Your purpose for our lives.

Though Your grace and mercy are patiently administered to us day by day, we don't truly recognize the work of Your hand. Even so, we have a deep desire to know You better, an irresistible need to draw near to You. Thank You for Your faithfulness and Your grace.

Help us to extend grace and mercy to each other in ways that reflect our awareness of all You have done for us. *Amen.*

One generation will commend Your works to another; they will tell of Your mighty acts.
~ Psalm 145:4 NIV ~

November 25

Good to Great!

Don't forget to do good and to share what you have with those in need, for such sacrifices are very pleasing to God.

~ Hebrews 13:16 ~

Lord, we enjoy the opportunity to help each other. Nothing does the heart so much good as surprising someone with a little unexpected gift or offering praise at just the right moment. In fact, those moments often move us from feeling good to feeling great!

Thank You for inspiring our hearts to reach out to others and do our best to help however we can. Thank You for the joy that You put into those moments so that they bring smiles to everyone.

Today, I pray for more people to do good simply because they can. I pray for those who will surprise themselves with their own generosity. *Amen.*

When God measures the greatness of an individual, He puts the tape measure around the heart, not the head.

~ Anonymous ~

November 26

Expecting an Answer

*May these words of my mouth and this meditation of
my heart be pleasing in Your sight, LORD.*
~ Psalm 19:14 NIV ~

Father, You who are all wisdom, all powerful and
knowing, beyond anything a mortal mind can comprehend, honor us by Your willingness to hear our
prayers. We come to You often in difficult times,
seeking Your direction because doing Your will is
important to us. Sometimes our prayers seem foolish or frivolous. The beautiful thing is that You hear
even those prayers and work to help us when we
pray with sincere hearts. The hard prayers, Lord,
are the ones where we feel desperate for an answer,
bowed down to the ground with sadness or heart-
break or disillusioned spirits. Those are the prayers
where we need to hear Your voice and where we
wait expectantly. *Amen.*

*None can believe how powerful prayer is,
and what it is able to effect, but those who
have learned it by experience.*
~ Martin Luther ~

November 27

Visions and Dreams

"Then after I have poured out My rains again, I will pour out My Spirit upon all people. Your sons and daughters will prophesy. Your old men will dream dreams. Your young men will see visions."

~ Joel 2:28 ~

Lord, help us to look for You in dreams and visions. Help us to seek Your face in all things so that we can prepare the way to You for others and help be Your hands and feet on this planet.

Grant us such a close connection with You so that we have greater sensitivity to Your voice and are more open to being guided by You even in our dreams. Pour out Your Spirit on us and let us be a beacon to people everywhere. Let us strive to achieve all Your goals in the work we do. *Amen.*

Cherish your visions and your dreams
as they are the children of your soul; the
blueprints of your ultimate achievements.
~ Napoleon Hill ~

November 28

A Little Witness

"Let your good deeds shine out for all to see, so that everyone will praise your heavenly Father."
~ Matthew 5:16 ~

Lord, You have given us an awesome task in allowing us to shine Your light for others. It's a wonderful task and sometimes it's extremely easy to do. But sometimes though, it's more difficult. Sometimes it feels like we're stepping into enemy camps and are not sure we can get out again safely.

Help us to share our faith by all the things we do. Let our lives be a witness to Your goodness and Your faithfulness. Let others see Your face through the work we do with our hands and feet. Help us to be the kind of walking influence that causes others to want to know more about You. *Amen.*

God has called us to shine. Let no one say that he cannot shine because he has not so much influence as some others may have. What God wants you to do is to use the influence you have.
~ Dwight L. Moody ~

It's a Gloomy Day!

*I am disgusted with my life. Let me complain freely. I
will speak in the bitterness of my soul.*
~ Job 10:1 ~

Lord, it's another one of those days when everything
seems to feel gray and cloudy. I can't seem to find
the sunshine no matter what I do or where I look.
Please help me to stand closer to Your light so that
I can see the good things that feel hidden from my
view. Release me from the shackles of sadness and
disgrace. Remind me of Your forgiveness and patience. Help me to find Your peace again.

I pray for all who suffer from depression in any
form. I pray that You lift their hearts and minds and
encourage them with Your steadfast love. In the
name of Jesus, I pray. *Amen.*

*Hear my cry for mercy as I call to You for help, as I
lift up my hands toward Your Most Holy Place.*
~ Psalm 28:2 NIV ~

November 30

*Give us grace, almighty Father, to address You
with all our hearts as well as with our lips.
You are present everywhere,
from You no secrets can be hidden.
Teach us to fix our thoughts on You,
reverently and with love,
so that our prayers are not in vain,
but are acceptable to You,
now and always,
through Jesus Christ our Lord.*

~ Jane Austen ~

December

Be Prepared!

"Know this: A homeowner who knew exactly when a burglar was coming would not permit the house to be broken into. You must be ready all the time, for the Son of Man will come when least expected."
~ Luke 12:39-40 ~

Father, grant us insight into the things that are important for us to know so that thieves can never come in the night and surprise us with their plans. Help us to be diligent and watchful over our homes and children, over our work and our relationships. More than anything, help us to be in constant communion with You so that we may be ready at any time to turn to You.

Bless those who are suffering from unexpected events that cause them grief, and bless all who seek to do their best to be prepared for life's array of circumstances. We ask for Your peace and mercy, in Christ's name. *Amen.*

The Lord watches over the way of the righteous,
but the way of the wicked will perish.
~ Psalm 1:6 *NIV* ~

Promises, Promises!

We are looking forward to the new heavens and the new earth He has promised, a world where everyone is right with God. And so, dear friends, while you are waiting for these things to happen, make every effort to live a pure and blameless life. And be at peace with God.

~ 2 Peter 3:13-14 ~

Father, how glorious it is that You have promised us such an amazing future! It is hard to imagine a place where everyone will be right with God and yet, it is a dazzling picture of hope and peace.

As this year comes to a close, help us to make the effort to live in ways that are pleasing to You. Help us seek to become holy and compassionate, patient and loving. You have served as our example and have given us a glimpse of what it means to live well and righteously. Help us to desire that kind of life more than we ever have before. *Amen.*

There is a living God. He has spoken in the Bible. He means what He says and will do all He has promised.

~ Hudson Taylor ~

December 2

Called out of Darkness!

This is so you can show others the goodness of God, for He called you out of the darkness into His wonderful light.

~ 1 Peter 2:9 ~

Lord of all light, thank You for Your tender mercy. Thank You for being our beacon on a hill that can be seen from anywhere we are. Thank You for calling us out of the darkness so we can be exposed to more of who You are and move closer to You each day.

We pray for more light to shine across this planet and that more of Your children would wake up to Your glorious Son-rise and know that You are the only true light of the world.

Thank You for showing us the way. Help us to let Your light shine within us wherever we go. *Amen.*

I would rather walk with God in the dark than go alone in the light.
~ Mary Gardiner Brainard ~

December 3

Sheltered in Love

So we fasted and earnestly prayed that our God would take care of us, and He heard our prayer.
~ Ezra 8:23 ~

Lord, when we turn to You as little children, running to Your arms for protection and love, we are grateful for Your tender mercy and nurturing presence.

Thank You for hearing our prayers and for taking such faithful care of our needs. You alone know what we need, what is important to our existence. You know when we need to simply rest in the protection of Your Spirit and Your comforting wings.

Bless Your children always with a place to go when they are fearful, and a place to rest when life makes them weary. Show them the power that comes through a relationship of mutual love and joy. *Amen.*

He will cover you with His feathers, and under His wings you will find refuge; His faithfulness will be your shield and rampart.
~ Psalm 91:4 NIV ~

December 4

Surprise and Delight!

*That night the LORD appeared to Solomon in a dream,
and God said, "What do you want? Ask, and I will
give it to you!"*

~ 1 Kings 3:5 ~

Father, it must have been amazing for Solomon to
awaken after his dream and realize that You had
offered to give him whatever he wanted. The gift of
his dreaming mind was that he knew what he most
needed. He knew that he was overwhelmed by the
prospect of being Israel's leader and that he needed
Your guidance and instruction to help him do the job
well.

Help us to also ask You for those things that not
only benefit our lives, but those things that benefit
everyone around us. Grant each of us the kind of
wisdom that brings others more mercy, peace, and
grace. *Amen.*

*Whoever is wise, let him heed these things
and consider the great love of the LORD.*
~ Psalm 107:43 NIV ~

Who Is God?

They will ask, "Which god are you talking about?
What is His name? Then what should I tell them?"
God replied, "I AM THE ONE WHO ALWAYS IS.
Just tell them, I AM has sent me to you."
~ Exodus 3:13-14 ~

God of all things, it is always difficult for human beings to try to understand how vast and how wide and how deep Your love really is. It is hard for us to truly contemplate Your power and Your generosity and infinite patience. We have tested You and tried You and forsaken You over and over again and yet, You remain faithful. We have disappointed You and run from You and yet You've stayed near, always willing to turn back to us when we seek Your face.

Lord, help us to know You. Help us to desire nothing more than to truly know You, our Creator, our Redeemer, and our constant and continual Friend. Thank You for always being with us. *Amen.*

Let everything that has breath praise the LORD.
~ Psalm 150:6 NIV ~

December 6

Discovering the Truth

"You are truly My disciples if you keep obeying My teachings. And you will know the truth, and the truth will set you free."

~ John 8:31-32 ~

Lord, I pray for all who seek You, who honor You with their lips and their hearts, to know the truth. I pray that Your Spirit would prevail and cause them to desire more of Your teachings and have greater opportunity to share a living truth that can set them free.

The world may not make any of this easy, but You have overcome the world and You have given us one path to discover truth. Thank You that we can embrace the love of Jesus and be comforted there. Bless all who seek You today. *Amen.*

For great is His love toward us, and the faithfulness of the LORD endures forever.
~ Psalm 117:2 NIV ~

The Gift of Peace

*How beautiful on the mountains are the feet of those
who bring good news of peace and salvation, the news
that the God of Israel reigns!*
~ Isaiah 52:7 ~

Lord, as we approach Christmas and the end of the
year, we seek the gifts to share with others that will
sustain them through the years ahead. We send out
good wishes and wrap brightly colored packages
with great excitement.

Today, I am made most aware of Your many gifts
to us, those gifts of mercy and grace and especially
of peace. Our hearts long for a sense of peace so that
our souls can rest perfectly in Your kind embrace. Be
with us, Lord, Emmanuel. Be with us and grant us
the irreplaceable gift of Your peace on this day and in
the days ahead. I ask You for this gift in Jesus' name.
Amen.

*The Lord is God, and He has
made His light shine upon us.*
~ Psalm 118:27 NIV ~

December 8

Wrapped in Grace

Blessed are those who have learned to acclaim You,
who walk in the light of Your presence, O Lord.
~ Psalm 89:15 NIV ~

Lord, there's nothing more exciting than knowing I am surrounded by Your grace, blanketed by Your love. Divine grace makes everything possible, makes every day bearable. You provide a canopy under which we can walk. You shade us from the things that might cause us to be doubtful. You light our way when we can no longer see the path.

You have outfitted us for life by simply surrounding us with all that You are and when we know this, we can't help but see You everywhere and in everything we do. I know that nothing else can satisfy my soul more than having Your faithful and continual help and guidance. You shower us with love and cause us to want more of Your light each day. I give You thanks and praise. *Amen.*

A state of mind that sees God in everything is
evidence of growth in grace and a thankful heart.
~ Charles G. Finney ~

December 9

Family Ties

"All the families of the earth will be blessed through you and your descendants. What's more, I will be with you, and I will protect you wherever you go."
~ *Genesis 28:14-15* ~

Father in heaven, You clearly set the stage for all of Your children to recognize You as the head of the family.

We are family! No matter where we live, or where we work, what our customs are or what our culture dictates, we are Your children. You gave us a lineage that goes on forever, protecting and guiding and nurturing our steps.

Help us to recognize each person we meet today as a member of our family, Your family. Help us to reach out in grace and love to those who walk the way with us in each small town, each big city, each place on earth. Thank You for giving us such strong family ties. *Amen.*

A family is a place where principles are hammered and honed on the anvil of everyday living.
~ *Chuck Swindoll* ~

December 10

Wrapping Things Up!

Be sure to do what you should, for then you will enjoy the personal satisfaction of having done your work well, and you won't need to compare yourself to anyone else. For we are each responsible for our own conduct.

~ Galatians 6:4-5 ~

Lord, as this year winds down to a close and I wrap up projects, I pray to finish those things well. I pray that I will honor You with the work I've put forward and to do a better job next year of doing those things You would have me do. Help me to further the work of Your kingdom. Help me to find fulfilment in knowing that I've done what I could to help others and to be generous with my time and resources.

As I consider the precious gift You gave to us at Christmas through Your Son, Jesus, I am inspired to seek more of You. I pray that I would be obedient to Your Word and generous to those around me. *Amen.*

Satisfy us in the morning with Your unfailing love,
that we may sing for joy and be glad all our days.
~ Psalm 90:14 NIV ~

What Are the Odds?

They will not labor in vain, for they will be a people blessed by the LORD.

~ Isaiah 65:23 *NIV* ~

Lord, we live at risk every day. The odds are good that we will fail at something today, whether it's failing to eat right, or failing to finish the work we assigned to ourselves. The odds are also good that we will be successful at something. We will finally complete a small task that has been on our list for some time, or we will actually spend time in prayer as we have meant to do.

Grant us now more courage to do the things You want us to accomplish. Give us true vision to inspire our steps and help us to fulfill our life purpose. Help us to understand that "risk" is not a bad concept, that taking a chance is sometimes the best possible opportunity to see Your hand at work as long as our motivations are pure. *Amen.*

Refuse to be average. Let your heart soar as high as it will.

~ A. W. Tozer ~

The Twelve Days
of Christmas

"Prepare the way for the LORD's coming! Clear the road for Him!"

~ Matthew 3:3 ~

Father, You are all things, Creator, Redeemer … all that is or ever was! Thank You for all You've done. Thank You for not giving up on us but instead, finding a way for us to be close to You again. Thank You for the gift of Your beloved Son.

Help all of us who celebrate the gifts of Christmas and who prepare for the coming of Jesus, to unite in one voice of praise to You, our heavenly Father. Bless our lives and melt our stubbornness. Bring us closer to You as we prepare for Christmas Day! *Amen.*

There is a God-shaped vacuum in the heart of every man which cannot be filled by any created thing, but only by God, the Creator, made known through Jesus.

~ Blaise Pascal ~

December 13

A Renewed Spirit

Those who become Christians become new persons.
They are not the same anymore, for the old life is gone.
A new life has begun!
    ~ 2 Corinthians 5:17 ~

Lord, Christmas is a season to cleanse the human spirit, to open it up to more light and love, to radiate the blessings and joy You have given each human being. You don't care where we've been. You simply embrace us so that we can take more certain steps into the future. You lead the way for us.

This Christmas season, please open the hearts of those who lead and guide and teach others. Please renew the spirits of those who have suffered loss and grief. Be our light and our heart's desire. Thank You for allowing us to always begin again. *Amen.*

The new life is life "in Christ."
    ~ Theodore Epp ~

Of Stars and Wonders

Watchman, how much longer until morning? When will the night be over?

~ Isaiah 21:11 ~

Lord, like the shepherds who waited in the darkness, who watched over the flocks, we wait for You. We wait for Your glorious star to shine and lead us forward. You have given us enough light to know the value of continuing to watch for Your grace and mercy in every area of our lives.

You leave us in continual awe and wonder and we see Your hand shape our lives in personal and loving ways. We see how You care for us and create new direction for us. You allow us to see Your hand in the things we do and to know our lives have meaning and value and purpose. You are the One we watch for, the One who makes the waiting worthwhile in every circumstance. We thank You and praise You forever. *Amen.*

Surely God is my help; the Lord is the One who sustains me.

~ Psalm 54:4 NIV ~

December 15

Simple Joys and Pure Hearts

"God blesses those whose hearts are pure, for they will see God."

~ Matthew 5:8 ~

Father, we come before You with childlike hearts and hopes. We know that to truly see You, we must step aside from the world and gaze humbly on the simple things that make life remarkable. It's hard to imagine what thoughts might have crossed the mind of Mary as she awaited the birth of the child she carried. Surely, it was more mystery than anything else to her to know that somehow You had chosen her to bring Jesus to live among us.

Help us now to come to You with pure hearts, simply for the joy of being in Your presence. *Amen.*

Purity of heart and simplicity are of great force with Almighty God, who is in purity most singular, and of nature most simple.

~ St. Gregory the Great ~

December 16

Prayer for Faith

Then Jesus prayed this prayer: "O Father, Lord of heaven and earth, thank You for hiding the truth from those who think themselves wise and clever, and for revealing it to the childlike. Yes, Father, it pleased You to do it this way!"

~ Matthew 11:25-26 ~

Lord, there's nothing more precious than seeing the face of a child beaming at the thought of a hoped-for gift at Christmas or taking part in the nativity play.

It's no wonder that You chose to offer Your love and grace to those who could see You in this way. Help us to seek You with the kind of enthusiasm that radiates with hope and washes over us like the blessings of Christmas morning. You brought us Your greatest gift at Christmas and we thank You that it doesn't take a scientific mind, or a brilliant scholar to see what You have done. It only takes one heart, fully trusting, fully accepting, and fully anticipating the fulfillment that only You can bring. *Amen.*

How priceless is Your unfailing love!
~ Psalm 36:7 NIV ~

December 17

Committed by Grace

"I know all the things you do, that you are neither hot nor cold. I wish you were one or the other! But since you are like lukewarm water, I will spit you out of My mouth!"

~ Revelations 3:15-16 ~

Father in heaven, the Christmas season gives us pause and cause to rethink our commitment to You. It gives us a chance to look carefully at our faith, and reach up to You. We so often go about our business with no real thought to how we might connect more fully with You and create a committed relationship.

At this season of great joy, let us take the time to recommit our spirits and our hearts to Your love and grace. You are our shining star, our everlasting joy! Help us to be fully connected to You in heart, body, and mind. *Amen.*

There are very few who in their hearts do not believe in God, but what they will not do is give Him exclusive right of way. They are not ready to promise full allegiance to God alone.

~ D. L. Moody ~

A Charitable Heart

All must give as they are able, according to the
blessings given to them by the LORD your God.
~ Deuteronomy 16:17 ~

Lord, I pray that we would all seek more opportunities to help those who are suffering from the chaos of life and whether we do charitable acts of kindness, or simply lift the spirit of another through a conversation or a good deed, that we would keep moving in that direction each day.

You need us to be Your hands and feet, Your eyes and ears, and sometimes even Your voice so that others might come to know You are there. Revive the embers of our charitable hearts so that we might be the light to many others as we enter the gates of a New Year. *Amen.*

Blessed is he who has regard for the weak;
the LORD delivers him in times of trouble.
~ Psalm 41:1 NIV ~

December 19

Our Heart's Desire

See how very much our heavenly Father loves us, for He allows us to be called His children, and we really are!

~ 1 John 3:1 ~

Lord, You have brought us to You, committed Your steadfast love so that we might be Your children, raised in faith and protected by grace.

You are truly our heart's desire! Help us then to be more willing to share our hope, the hope we know that cannot be found anywhere else on earth, except in You. Help us to speak of You often, to trust You completely, and to reach out in Your name. Everything on this planet is Yours and every person here is part of Your creation, part of Your divine idea. Grant that all of us might be more determined and zealous for You so that we might stand tall as "children of light." *Amen.*

It is still one of the tragedies of human history that the "children of darkness" are frequently more determined and zealous than the "children of light."
~ Martin Luther King, Jr. ~

Devout and Devoted

*"If you look for Me in earnest, you will find Me when
you seek Me. I will be found by you," says the LORD.*
~ Jeremiah 29:13-14 ~

Lord, around the time of the birth of Jesus, some were earnestly looking for You. Astronomers had been diligently studying the stars looking for any sign of Your coming. Mary was pondering the words of an angel in her heart and Joseph was in awe of all that was unfolding before him.

For all those who earnestly strive to hear Your voice, I pray that You would help them to find You. For all those who diligently study the Scriptures or seek You in prayer, I pray that You would move across the great abyss that separates them from You and bring them close. For all who still look for signs and hope to hear the voices of angels declaring Your presence, I pray that their ears might be opened to You. *Amen.*

True and living devotion presupposes the love of God.
~ Francis de Sales ~

What's in a Name?

"You will become pregnant and have a son, and you are to name Him Jesus. He will be very great and will be called the Son of the Most High."
~ Luke 1:31-32 ~

Dear Lord, we have been taught that there is no other name under heaven through which we may be saved and so we are ever grateful.

You have shown us that names mean something to You. The name of Jesus means everything to those who believe. He has been called Emmanuel, "God with us," and the Light of the World and the Savior. In an effort to describe how much He means to us, we have sought to give Him a name. Bless the name of the Lord and bless our lives as we learn each day to follow Him more closely in the days ahead. In the name of our life-giving Savior we pray. *Amen.*

Glory in His holy name; let the hearts of those who seek the LORD rejoice.
~ Psalm 105:3 NIV ~

Holy, Holy, Holy!

In a great chorus they sang, "Holy, holy, holy is the Lord Almighty! The whole earth is filled with His glory!"

~ Isaiah 6:3 ~

Lord, as we prepare to offer You praise and thanks and come to You singing, "O Holy Night," let us be reminded about the true meaning of holiness. Let us be in awe of Your very nature which is the only thing that will ever be truly holy. Help us understand what You want from us in terms of learning about being holy. We are so blind!

Father, we thank You for giving us Your light in the form of Your infant Son, that we might grow up with Him in true holiness and be Your sons and daughters as well. Thank You for guiding us on the path so we might attain more of You with each step we take. *Amen.*

Christ is the most perfect image of God, into which we are so renewed as to bear the image of God, in knowledge, purity, righteousness, and true holiness.
~ John Calvin ~

Angels We Have
Heard on High

Suddenly, the angel was joined by a vast host of others – the armies of heaven – praising God: "Glory to God in the highest heaven, and peace on earth to all whom God favors."

~ Luke 2:13-14 ~

Father in heaven, at Christmastime, we often contemplate the message of angels and that message reminds us that Jesus was born into the world for each of us, that none of us should be lost.

I pray that those voices of angels would still be heard loud and clear by all who have ears to hear and who seek His light. Thank You for Your gifted messengers who serve You and who serve humankind with their glorious presence. Help us to hear their voices and to respond in like manner with our own songs of joy and praise. Hallelujah! *Amen.*

Who is He, this King of glory?
The Lord Almighty – He is the King of glory.

~ Psalm 24:10 NIV ~

December 24

Birth Announcement

And while they were there, the time came for her baby to be born. She gave birth to her first child, a son. She wrapped Him snugly in strips of cloth and laid Him in a manger, because there was no room for them in the village inn.

~ Luke 2:6-7 ~

Lord God, we raise our voices in joy and thankfulness at the birth of Your dear Son. We thank You for loving us so much that You wanted us to have a living example of who You are.

You who could have demanded our obedience through great power, who could have cursed us for our sinfulness and left us to our own devices, instead, sent Light. We celebrate the Christ of Christmas, the Light of the world and the blessed and glorious Son of God. In praise and glory forever! *Amen.*

You have made known to me the path of life;
You will fill me with joy in Your presence,
with eternal pleasures at Your right hand.
~ Psalm 16:11 NIV ~

December 25

The Christmas Message

"I bring you good news of great joy for everyone! The Savior – yes, the Messiah, the Lord – has been born tonight in Bethlehem, the city of David!"
~ Luke 2:10-11 ~

Lord, even before we knew we needed a Savior, You found a way to save us. Even before we begged for mercy, You were merciful. You have always been ahead of us, seeking ways to embrace us and to give us an example of what love really is.

Bless all the babies born this day and each day. Bless those who come into this life with a sense of You and a purpose that would make their light shine as they grow. Bless those who bring hope to their families and those who are not certain why they are here. Each one is Your child. Each one has been touched by Your embrace because of Your one and only Son, Jesus. *Amen.*

For You created my inmost being; You knit me together in my mother's womb. I praise You because I am fearfully and wonderfully made.
~ Psalm 139:13-14 NIV ~

December 26

Hope of the World

I pray that your hearts will be flooded with light so that you can understand the wonderful future He has promised to those He called.

~ Ephesians 1:18 ~

Lord, thank You that You have not abandoned us to broken hearts, but have lifted us up and given us hope. Thank You for calling us into a future that is rich with promise and bright with the light of possibility. We know that in You all things are possible and that You are even now working out what is best for each of us as we walk with You each day.

I pray for all people everywhere who place their hope in You. I pray that their hearts would indeed be flooded with light so they can know You in a new way as this year ends and a new one begins. I pray that they would let go of any defeats they may have experienced in this year, and trust You for all they need today and always. *Amen.*

But as for me, I will always have hope;
I will praise You more and more.

~ Psalm 71:14 NIV ~

Grace and Glory

*May God, who gives this patience and encourage-
ment, help you live in complete harmony with each
other – each with the attitude of Christ Jesus toward
the other. Then all of you can join together with one
voice, giving praise and glory to God, the Father of our
Lord Jesus Christ.*

~ Romans 15:5-6 ~

Lord, sometimes we catch a glimpse of glory in a
beautiful sunset or a vista from scaling a mountain-
top. Sometimes we recognize those among us who
are heroes in one way or another and so we glory in
their acts of bravery or kindness.

Help us as we enter this New Year to set our priorities so that we take the time to glorify Your name
in all we do. Help us to focus our spirits in such a
way that we balance the efforts of our work life,
family life, and spiritual life. We pray that we would
do all things for Your grace and glory. *Amen.*

*Not to us, O LORD, not to us but to Your name be
the glory, because of Your love and faithfulness.*

~ Psalm 115:1 NIV ~

December 28

Looking Ahead

"So don't worry about tomorrow, for tomorrow will bring its own worries. Today's trouble is enough for today."

~ *Matthew 6:34* ~

Lord, as we close out the old year and head toward the new, remind us that all we really have is today. Today is the opportunity, the gift we have, the present is where we live. Help us to adjust our thinking so that we make this day worthwhile, learning those things that benefit us now, and grasping those things that pave the way for a brighter tomorrow.

Grant that we would taste and feel and touch the events of each day in meaningful ways. Grant that we would strive to a greater understanding of what it means to be Your children so that if no tomorrow comes, we can be content with what we did today. Bless all who put their lives in Your hands. *Amen.*

The fear of the Lord is the beginning of wisdom; all who follow His precepts have good understanding. To Him belongs eternal praise.

~ *Psalm 111:10 NIV* ~

In God We Trust

Our hope is in the living God, who is the Savior of all people and particularly of those who believe.
~ *1 Timothy 4:10* ~

Father, help us as we leave the old year behind to understand more than ever before, that we do have hope in You, our loving and living God. Help us know that no matter what the future holds, we can trust You to hold on to each of us. We can trust You to shelter us when we're feeling unprotected, to keep us safe when the path is uncertain before us.

We are fearful beings. It's interesting that when angels appeared to people through the Scriptures, they most often had to assure them not to be afraid. Help us to not be afraid as we look at the year ahead, and to put all our trust in You. *Amen.*

When I am afraid, I will trust in You.
~ *Psalm 56:3 NIV* ~

December 30

Endings and Beginnings

"I am the Alpha and the Omega, the First and the Last, the Beginning and the End."
~ Revelation 22:13 ~

Lord, we come to the close of another year. We step out of our old clothes, our old thinking, our old behaviors that do not serve You, and ask that You would renew us, and cause us to be ready to begin again. Give us the power of our faith to shine a light so bright that others would see us coming from far away. Help us to be the gospel for those who do not yet know You. Help us to be grace for those who seek understanding.

You are the beginning and the end and we are Your creation, Your children, and the offspring of Your Spirit. Grant us wisdom as we wait for Your return. Help us to be strong in our faith and to know that You are with us always, even to the end of this age. In the name of our Lord and Savior, we pray.

Amen.

Awake, my soul! I will awaken the dawn.
~ Psalm 57:8 ~